BEFRIENDING DEATH

BEFRIENDING DEATH

Over 100 Essayists on Living and Dying

MICHAEL VOCINO and ALFRED G. KILLILEA

BEFRIENDING DEATH
OVER 100 ESSAYISTS ON LIVING AND DYING

iUniverse books may be ordered through booksellers or by contacting:

iUniverse
1663 Liberty Drive
Bloomington, IN 47403
www.iuniverse.com
1-800-Authors (1-800-288-4677)

ISBN: 978-1-4917-3810-8 (sc)
ISBN: 978-1-4917-4057-6 (hc)
ISBN: 978-1-4917-3809-2 (e)

Library of Congress Control Number: 2014912383

Printed in the United States of America.

iUniverse rev. date: 07/21/2014

Michael Vocino dedicates this book to his pal, Joe.

Alfred Killilea dedicates this book to his wife, Mary Ann.

We want to begin this book with a note of gratitude to our authors. Without their willingness to join in this project our efforts would be for naught. We'd also like to thank Danielle Dirocco who gave us invaluable editorial assistance.

Contents

Chapter 3: Our Relationships Are More Important Than Our Mortality

Chapter 4: Views On The Necessity Of Faith

Chapter 8: Death And Appreciating Life

INTRODUCTION

In the Face of Death: Finding Meaning in Life

"Live your own life because you will die your own death."
—Latin Aphorism

Introduction—In the Face of Death: Finding Meaning in Life

This book comprises the collective wisdom of over 100 thoughtful people who were asked to respond in one page to this question: "In the face of death, how do you find meaning and fulfillment in life?"

It is not easy to speak about death in our culture. As children of revolution, we think of our country as young, energetic and future oriented. Our ideals of progress and vigor seem contradicted by the concept of death. But in a pluralistic culture of diverse ethnic traditions, our common mortality is perhaps the most powerful part of our story and it potentially unites everyone of us. The silence about death in America is a lost opportunity for people to find insight and support in walking "that lonesome valley."

This book provides brief essays from people of a vast array of backgrounds, all taking death seriously and openly reflecting on how and where they find meaning in life. While some of these writers come from other continents and from across the United States, many of these voices are from the smallest state, Rhode Island, which we feel serves as a microcosm of the diversity and insight of the larger country. This chance for a rare sharing of views on a truly profound subject has attracted commentators who are deeply religious and those who are not religious, noted authors and people who have never published a word, people celebrated by the world and people ignored by the world. As they are all equal in their mortality, they are equal in striving for an authentic existence and an honest description of what for them constitutes fulfillment. While our commitment as editors to inclusiveness inevitably results in essays that vary in power and polish, the reader will find in this book views about life and death from a true cross-section of our culture.

Preview of the Essays

Because there is such a wide variety of ways in which our authors have responded to our single question, "In the face of death, how do you find meaning and fulfillment in life," the essays defy simple categorization. Some common themes emerge, however. Some contributors believe that the only meaning that death allows in life is that derived from a theological perspective. Essays by David Dooley, Michael Cerbo, Bishop Thomas Tobin, Thomas Keefe and others find faith essential in looking death in the eye. Other contributors believe just the opposite, that a focus on an afterlife robs this life of significance and authenticity. Many other essayists do not take a position on religion and an afterlife and imply that what is a decisive support in contemplating death to some people is irrelevant to their view of life and death.

Some writers cite the creative process as what permits them to be uncowed by death. The Pulitzer Prize winning fiction writer Jhumpa Lahiri says she is most alive when writing and that it is a kind of little death each time she has to stop. Jacques Choron in his book, *Death and Western Thought*, is a critic of the idea that creativity can stand up to death. He argues that all creative works eventually perish and can constitute only a temporary memorial. Some of our authors would challenge Choron's emphasis on endurance as irrelevant to a person's transcending time-boundness in self-expression.

Many authors cite our relationships with others as providing meaning and fulfillment in the face of death. With Plato and Aristotle, these writers see our essence as social beings trumping the description of humans as mortal beings. It is interesting to observe that people who today turn to cryogenics or to the possibilities of organ renewal to solve the problem of death and to find immortality, rarely extend that quest to those who are close to them. The loneliness and self-centeredness of the immortalists would be an uninteresting Faustian swap for many of the essayists in this book. David Schock observes: "If love is real then death is nothing," and Cynthia Weisbord says: "We defy death by love." Josh Feinman argues that "all that really matters are your relationships." Timothy Heffernan finds deep meaning in "weaving the tapestries of family and community." Jane McCarthy finds a striking admonition in our mortality: "seek peace with your adversaries."

A theme that is embraced repeatedly in these essays is that it is the journey that is far more engaging and attractive than the destination in life. Gerald Kubasiak quotes a popular song in his essay: "Where you've been is good and gone, all you keep is the getting there." Ashley Stoehr says: "My fulfillment in life stems from a lack of fear or concern for an epilogue, only the present storyline matters. There is no happily ever after, merely the journey's final drink, but that last sip will be glorious." Winifred Brownell urges us to wake every morning like Scrooge discovering that he has another chance.

Some writers see the importance of being aware of our mortality but that underscores for them the greater importance of the awareness of life. Cheryl Foster has a playful skeleton dangling from her car mirror but notes: "We know that death's coming...but life beckons now." Similarly, Ilana Coenen, perhaps our youngest writer at 21, concludes: "I don't understand death, but life is too short to be afraid. I will not hide from the unknown. I will not ask myself when I will die or when death will come into my life again. But I will ask myself, am I living?"

The paradox of how reflecting on death thrusts us back to an appreciation of life is a theme that reverberates through most of the essays in this book. The ironic interplay of death and life is well captured by Jhumpa Lahiri's quote from the Italian poet, Umberto Saba: "And it's the thought of death that helps us, after all, to live." Susan Matarese writes: "I think that the consciousness of death has helped me to live more mindfully, to focus on the present rather than dwelling on the past or worrying about the future." This irony runs deep in Dan Novak's claim that "Death becomes an ally, friend, companion." and in Barnaby McLaughlin's conclusion that "all life exists only because of death." B. L. Headtinkerwalla argues that "death means life" and Joseph Creedon urges us to "befriend death." Gerhard Müller sees in each death a birth.

Even in a set of essays that react to the very hard challenge of losing someone precious, there is the irony of death affirming life. Evelyn Wight tells of the struggle to "keep going" after the murder of her sister. "Sometimes I still sob for hours, or days. But for me, life has been made worth living by continuing to find things to love. I press my animal body toward warmth. I forgive myself for surviving. I laugh out loud at silliness. I marvel at butterflies and concrete."

While each essay in this book is unique, together they present a tapestry of courage, struggle, and insight. It is fascinating and humbling to see the many different ways people can respond to the same question and to realize how much we can learn from these many varied perspectives. At a time when we are often overwhelmed by the eagerness of people to provide their opinions on politics and sports, here is a rare opportunity to hear people share their most profound views on life and death.

Alfred Killilea
Michael Vocino
Kingston, Rhode Island

Readers are invited to submit comments or brief essays of their own to mortalityandmorality@etal.uri.edu.

CHAPTER ONE

The Journey Is What Counts

"Our birth is nothing but our death begun."
—Edward Young

John J. Barry–I Might As Well Die Alive

Given the bizarre self-serving pictures man-made religion paints of the afterlife, it looks to me like this life is the only game in town. (I do pray I'm wrong). So if this life is all I got and death is the final act, the best I can hope for is a slow mortification of the flesh. This will give me an opportunity to show my kids how to die right like Mimi in La Boheme singing a beautiful aria while dying of consumption. Alternatives are get hit by a bus, die while saving kids from a burning building or dementia.

As a spiritually limited atheist, I suspect the desire to do good is a Darwinian survival trait. It would be great to be admired—ok, I'll settle for liked. Unfortunately I've run out of time to discover the cure for cancer or to create a bumper sticker that will bring peace in our time. So the best I can hope for is a legacy that influences my kids and maybe future grand kids for the good of the tribe. A small ripple of values across a few years. Not so great, eh? But as Harriet McBryde Johnson, a wheelchair bound advocate for the disabled said, "When I die, I might as well die alive." That's the plan. I know life laughs at our plans but if the world is a better place for my being part of it I'm good to go.

Jack Barry writes of his biography:

"By some accounts I should have been a sexually conflicted, substance abusing, and small time B&E man. I grew up on welfare in a single parent home, in a housing project in the hard part of Hartford, CT. There were few male role models. Growing up in a black and white neighborhood showed me early-on that life was seldom black and white. Dysfunction, self-destruction and professional victimhood abounded. I was not only exposed to it, I was immersed in it. But that account ignores some fundamentals.

Looking back I think I did manage to get a few things right. As near as I can figure, here's why. My mother's unconditional love gave me security, optimism and the ability to love (if not the wisdom to profess it early and often). Her hard work gave me a strong work ethic and perseverance. I learned about loyalty from her every day sacrifice. I also believe the world is a better place because there were times I did not get caught. I take no credit in what luck has brought me. But I do take credit for being wise enough to enjoy it while I can."

Ross Cheit–Finding Meaning in Battling Hate, Suffering and Injustice

The question is as generous as it is challenging. It is generous because it presumes that one has found meaning and fulfillment in life. It is challenging not only because of the word limit but also because of the predicate about death. My generation, part of the baby boom, arguably denies or ignores death more than it faces it. Working with college-age students compounds that problem. I am surrounded by boundless idealism, energy, and good health. We do not talk much about death at the university and there is little interest in things like Social Security. Those caveats aside, I find tremendous fulfillment in teaching students who want to make the world a better place. Their hopes and dreams are inspiring and nourishing. I also find fulfillment in small, simple moments: in my kayak, at the yoga studio, or walking the neighborhood with my wife. But I am afraid that the meaning of all this is less clear to me with time. There is so much inexplicable hate, suffering and injustice in the world. Trying to do something about that seems meaningful to me. Trying to reconcile such problems with the idea of some grand design or purpose is beyond my understanding.

Professor Ross Cheit joined the faculty of Brown University in 1986, coming to Brown from UC-Berkeley where he received his law degree and a Ph.D. in public policy. His graduate work revolved around regulatory agencies and issues of insurance and risk, leading to his book, Setting Safety Standards. In recent years, Professor Cheit has been working on a book at the intersection of law, psychology and political science. Cheit also works on issues related to ethics in government and he is currently the chair of the Rhode Island Ethics Commission.

Ilana Coenen—Death Is My Constant

Death is my constant. It's been a surrounding force in my life for over seven years. At 21, that's 1/3 of my existence. From funeral to funeral, I have heard every answer about the meaning of life and each condolence. I have heard of heaven. I don't buy it, never have. "There is nothing to see at the bottom of the sky or this heaven." I don't believe in heaven nor do I believe in god, but I am open. Open to believing I am not all that is. I respect what's around me. I seek refuge in its beauty. I sit in front of the ocean on the hood of my car, sunshine hits my face. Something tells me that there is more than what meets the eye. When feeling love, loss, joy, or pain, we experience something that engulfs us. It goes beyond us as personalities inside a body.

I don't wish to live forever, only once. In that period, I wish to truly live. How do I find adversity and meaning in life after spending 1/3 of it mourning the dead? I live a conscious life.

I give what I can, sometimes what I cannot. I love openly and try living selflessly. I do this knowing that I will die and these acts may have been worthless. I do this without hope of finding heaven or meeting god. These acts make me feel that I am a part of something larger than myself. They make me feel alive.

I thought I knew death. I saw it as some distant relative that comes around at times. I don't understand death, but life is too short to be afraid. I will not hide from the unknown. I will not ask myself when I will die or when death will come into my life again. But I will ask myself, am I living?

Ilana Coenen grew up in the Hudson Valley of New York and now resides in Providence, R.I. after graduating from the University of Rhode Island. She finds inspiration in traveling, exploring and creating works of art through lost and forgotten items. In the future, Ilana hopes to work with a nonprofit in an effort to enhance the lives of others by spreading karuna and sharing some of the beauty absorbed through her life experiences.

Sandra Enos—Some Final Thoughts

When I am laid to rest
Passed away
Gone to the other side
I would hope that my friends would encircle me with
Those things that have surrounded me every day.

I would rather my coffin be dotted with wild asters
And mildewed hostas than draped with tropical flowers
Whose journey to my grave is longer than any I have taken.
I want no showy flower heads, with bright orange beaks
All that vulgar beauty
I want no flowers that like some relatives
only show up at funerals.

Perhaps, some beloved seaweed
Spent sea grass.
A tide's collection of bleached shells.
Maybe, if I pass away in deep autumn
A branch from the holly bush
Its red berries in bloom.

Or maybe, my partner's favorite flower, not mine
For the gesture is for the living, not the dead.
For the comfort of feeling that one has loved as well as one could.
I would hope that there would be no talk about my soul
Returning to its maker.
I would dream that someone would preach that my soul
Like all others
Joined together many stolen parts.

All my life I have taken measure for my own
Of what I have believed to be
The essence of those I knew and loved.
The kindness of some
The compassion of others

The tenderness they shared
The lives, those ineffable moments we lived.
When they lay me down with pieces of them
Elements of many others
I have the warmth and the beat of their hearts with me.

Sandra Enos has spent her 64 years in a variety of pursuits ranging from college professor in New England to a construction supervisor in rural Alabama. As some young women provide for a future life in their hope chests, Enos has collected a lifetime's worth of journals and diaries—all waiting for sorting out. A memoirist, humorist, playmate, and photographer, she is embracing that time in life where one's left-brained dominance takes a long retreat and allows a fuller richer appreciation of the magnificence of the natural and created world to emerge.

Joanne Fahey—Dying Long Before a Last Breath

This question has provoked much thought and reflection and always with the same outcome. Life's meaning for me unfolds gradually, day by day, experience by experience. Fulfillment is found in living each day as if it were my last. Some days I am more successful at this than others. In the Book of Deuteronomy, the second book of the Bible, God says, "I set before you life and death; choose life." This is my personal philosophy, that guiding principle which affects every decision I make, no matter how important or how insignificant that decision is. Always I ask myself: Is this choice life-giving or death-producing? Life-giving choices bring greater freedom, deeper peace and the reassurance that I am living life to the full. Death-producing decisions imprison me; bury me under layers and layers of untruths and illusions. Death-producing choices pay homage to my false self and all that is less than I can be and become. Death-producing decisions lead to stagnation, apathy, indifference and mediocrity. There are so many ways in which death entraps us. We are quite capable of dying long before we draw our last breath.

And so, in the face of imminent death, I would choose life. Choosing life is about being faithful to the ordinary events that fill my days. It is about healing broken relationships; it is about forgiveness, which includes self-forgiveness; it is about attentiveness to people in my life; it is about having a cup of coffee with a friend; it is about tending the garden and doing the laundry; it is about speaking out against injustices and assuming responsibility for my life. I choose life when I am faithful to my prayer and when I take a walk with a child I choose life when I offer a listening ear or a shoulder to cry on. In ever so many ordinary ways, too numerous to mention, I choose life.

This is how I strive to live each day. In the face of imminent death, I would choose to do nothing different.

Sister Joanne Fahey was elected to the leadership team of the Sisters of the Cross and Passion. She was involved in education during her early career, teaching in schools staffed by her community in New York, Connecticut, and Rhode Island. In 1985 she responded to her community's call to establish a mission in Jamaica, West Indies remaining there for two years. Upon her return from Jamaica, Sister Joanne became involved in the ministry of Spiritual Direction.

Cheryl Foster—Life Beckons Now

I keep a totem in my car: a cheerful rubbery skeleton dangling in front of a car. It hangs off the rearview mirror. The ball began life as an air freshener but has long been bereft of its scent.

That skeleton, it's where we're all headed. It's where we're all at. I think it no bad thing to meditate on the embedded fact of mortality each and every day, to face up and for real to the end that we carry from birth. There's no doubt that it's coming.

And yet still, and yet still, and yet still, and yet still—we breathe now. Today comes only once, observed Schopenhauer; but we're too often inclined to waste it.

A thousand gay and pleasant hours are wasted in ill-humor; we let them slip by unenjoyed, and sigh for them in vain when the sky is overcast. Those present moments that are bearable, be they never so trite and common,—passed by in indifference, or, it may be, impatiently pushed away,—those are the moments we should honor…

Let the disco begin! Each day is a little life, thought Schopenhauer; every waking and rising a little birth, every fresh morning a little youth, every going to rest and sleep a little death.

My totem keeps me focused, forcing me to reckon with the paradoxical dance between Being and Nothing within it. A dance we can lead while alive, while a heart beats within us.

That skeleton bobs to the rhythms. We know that death's coming. But life beckons now.

Cheryl Foster is Professor of Philosophy and Associate Director of the Honors Program at the University of Rhode Island, where she specializes in theoretical and applied aesthetics, environmental philosophy and theories of knowledge, including controversies in art as well as environmental dilemmas and decision-making. In addition to her writing, teaching and advising, Professor Foster co-hosts The Beauty Salon, a weekly talk-format radio show about all things aesthetic in the state of Rhode Island. In 2013 she was one of 7 educators nationally to receive the Kennedy Center/ Stephen Sondheim Inspirational Teacher Award.

Carol Gibbons—Meaning in Death From Meaning in Life

Really, I have not had to face death very often. My father died 3 years ago of bladder cancer at age 91, and a dear companion John died last year of pancreatic cancer at age 70. My father fought the idea that he was dying, while John accepted it with equanimity. Both began prescribed treatments with positive attitudes. My father's difficulty with his impending death was related to his concern for my mother's welfare after he was gone. Both my parents were still in their own home, and my father was active as a volunteer with the church, alumni organizations, and Meals on Wheels (even at his age). He was the one who did the grocery shopping, drove to doctor's appointments, even did laundry and housework. He felt needed. My siblings and I assured him that we would be there for Mom, and she had already decided to move to assisted living once he was gone. She wanted to be the first to die, and was unhappy that that would not be the case. She is now 94, and is content, but does not see any purpose to her life, even though my siblings and I visit often and she enjoys being with us.

John had led a very full life. An academic, he had traveled widely, mentored many students in doctoral studies, and raised two sons. His wife had died of cancer two years before I met him, and we had a wonderful relationship until he died. He was optimistic, yet realistic, about his chances of survival. We continued to enjoy concerts, theater, travel, family and friends throughout his chemo treatment time.

How do you find meaning in life in the face of death? I think it is the same way you find meaning in life in general. You think back on happy memories; you hope you have made a positive difference in the lives of some of the people you have met; you are grateful for the positive difference people have made in your own life. I have children who are raising their own families now, and are self-sufficient and productive. I think I could face a diagnosis of death knowing that they are OK.

Carol Gibbons has taught mathematics at Salve Regina University in Newport, R.I., for the past 24 years. She is the mother of 6 children and grandmother of 8. She loves the Rhode Island beaches, has enjoyed traveling to such locales as Tahiti and Japan, and has spent many years as a volunteer for the local opera company. She has also worked to advocate for women as a member of the R.I. Commission on Women.

David Gitlitz—Not Yet

Back from the brink: you've asked me to reflect
on what it's meant to flirt with the abyss.
Yet, don't we all? This fleshy edifice
will fall. If life's the cause, death's the effect.

My parent's perfect gift had one defect:
one protease inhibitor it missed,
making my body its own nemesis,
wracking my lungs, leaving my liver wrecked.

And then a friend stepped up and gave me half
his liver, freeing me to draw away
from the abyss, to celebrate the debt

that we each owe to life: to love, to laugh,
to serve, to make full use of every day,
to greet each deathless dawn smiling, "Not yet…"

David Gitlitz is a lifelong wanderer, with an academic career at several universities in the US and abroad and in several capacities (teacher, chair, dean, provost), and has written books, often in conjunction with his wife Dr. Linda Davidson, on literature, Sephardic history, anthropology, pilgrimage studies, and culinary history. Now professor emeritus of Hispanic Studies at the University of Rhode Island, unencumbered by committee meetings and student papers, Gitlitz continues to write and travel. You can find him in Rhode Island (summer), Mexico (winter), or on the road (spring and fall), and always at www.gitlitzdavidson.com. Not all who wander are lost.

Gale Greenleaf—Living the Way You Want to Die

A few years ago, over a few days, I watched my father dying. By the time I got to his bedside, he was sliding rapidly away, physically, mentally—and emotionally. I wanted to give him whatever love and support I could, in spite of our often thorny and unsatisfying (to me, anyway) relationship, but there was little I could do. It hurt me to see him pick at his bedclothes and move restlessly in his bed, and ask for water when the doctors had forbidden it. (I did finally decide that was nonsense and gave him water. What possible difference could it make?) The experience taught me that the end is too late to think about the end. Since then my increased awareness of my own mortality, having lost a part of myself, has motivated me to be more forgiving, less impatient, and more conscious of my indebtedness and interconnectedness to other people.

If I found out I were dying, my first priority would be to let everyone I appreciate and love know it. That might mean simply saying "I love you" to some who, hopefully, already know it. For other people it would take more subtlety to express appreciation in a way that didn't leave people feeling awkward, as if I were expecting reciprocation. So I am practicing every day how to express affection and gratitude in ways that make people happy and comfortable. The way I'm trying to live now is the way I want to die.

Gale Robin Greenleaf added her middle name when she was 11, then legally invented her last name after her second divorce. She is a 66-year-old former hippie, professional fiddler and singer, and offset press woman. She received her Ph.D. at 56 and taught technical writing to unwilling engineers at the University of Texas at Austin until she gleefully retired to Brunswick, Maine, last year. She gardens, travels, loves animals, and has a century-old project house in Jonesport, Maine.

Gerald E. Kubasiak—All You Keep Is the Getting There

"**D**id an angel whisper in your ear, hold you close and take away your fears, in your long last moments," the lyrics by singer-songwriter Lucinda Williams in her song "Lake Charles." My belief is that "in the face of death" the meaning you find in your life will relieve your fears. Your "meaning" comes from the relationship you've had with others, your spouse, children, siblings, friends and professional colleagues. A friend contemplating his obituary (but not facing death) stated that it should only say, "Paul was born on (date), did the best he could, and died on (date)." The test is whether we did the best we could have done in our relationships. Did we truly share love? I have a wife of 46+ years and daughter with whom I have a parent as well as a professional relationship. I had parents who loved and cared for me. I've had a long professional career which has allowed me to touch and be touched by the lives of many people. "In the face of death," I will look upon those relationships. I hope that the whispers will tell me that I did the best I could have with those relationships. At that point I will hope to find meaning and peace. After all in the words of one more singer-songwriter, Townes Van Zandt (from "To Live is to Fly"), "where you've been is good and gone, all you keep is the getting there."

Gerald Kubasiak is a 73-year-old active practicing lawyer, dedicated reader of economic and political history and collector of historical maps. He is also currently serving as a judge on the Illinois Court of Claims. He has successfully continued a marriage of 47 years (and counting) and practices law with his daughter. He maintains that Robert Caro's "The Years of Lyndon Johnson," series (still in process) is the best political history ever written.

Daniel Larsh—The Path to Death Defines Us

Since the days of my childhood, I have been fascinated by the R.M.S. Titanic. A young man who was traveling on the Titanic was offered a seat in a lifeboat. It happened to be his birthday the day the ship sank. He told the officer, "Today, I'm a man, so I'm going to stay behind with the rest of the men." He perished during the sinking.

Would I have the courage to do the same thing in the face of death? Death is part of what makes us human; it's inevitable and we cannot fight it. The journey leading up to our end contains the answers to these questions. It's up to individuals to select the one that defines them.

Daniel Larsh is a 2013 graduate of the University of Rhode Island where he studied Film Media and Communication. He resides in Rhode Island and is currently a Video Editor at the URI Graduate School of Oceanography. Daniel is actively pursuing a career as an independent filmmaker. He is passionately focussing the spotlight on numerous subjects including the ocean, humanities, and his home.

Bernice Lott—The Golden Rule of a Socialist, Secularist, Atheist

Growing older has not changed my views or feelings about "the meaning of life" or how I find fulfillment. Perhaps this will change as the prospect of death looms closer and is imminent but, as of now, I still find the phrase "meaning in life" not meaningful and would be hard pressed to come up with a simple response. I can do better with "fulfillment in life." For me, it comes from the pursuit of pleasure and joy in family and work. Despite the inevitable frustrations and disappointments, it is the process that is energizing and rewarding along with the hope of possibilities for positive outcomes. The same is true of my commitment to social justice and progressive socioeconomic change to advance human health and welfare. I am an old-fashioned proponent of the "golden rule" and an unreconstructed socialist, secularist, and atheist. I believe that experience shapes how we behave and what we believe and that we should do whatever we can to maximize the goodness and beneficial nature of that experience for ourselves, those we care about, and all others. Art and theater, the beauty to be found in nature, advances in empirical science, and fair access to the resources of society are all elements in fostering "the good life."

Bernice Lott, born in 1930, is the mother of three, grandmother of seven, and wife of Al. She remains actively involved with social psychological research and writing and is committed to the exploration of the significance in peoples' life experiences of gender, social class, ethnicity, and sexual identification. She has traveled widely, taught at universities in Colorado, Kentucky, and Hawaii, and done sabbatical research in Japan, New Zealand, and California.

William F. McDonald—How to Assess a Life

Looking backwards at our lives, they can have a deceptive sense of fate about them. Sometimes it seems that things <u>had</u> to happen the way they did. But then, you look closer and you remember all the contingencies, the forks in the road, the choices…and you end up being amazed you ever got anywhere.

Also, when trying to judge the value of one's life, there is a tendency to conflate all the good and the bad times, all the triumphs and the regrets, and to think in terms of some overall average. But, as I explain to the students in my statistics course, averages are deceptive. A man can have his head in the oven and his feet in the refrigerator and can honestly say that "on the average" he feels pretty good.

Then there are those comparisons that are often the reason for going to or avoiding class reunions. So what, if any, is the significance of the fact that you came out at the top or on the bottom or in the middle of your class? What if you did not do most of the things on your bucket list? What difference does it make?

I recommend Ken Burns' advice to a college graduating class. When judging the merits of your life, you should pick those events, achievements and habits of the heart that give you the greatest joy and solace, that strike you as good examples of wisdom, leadership, generosity and love.

Bill McDonald is a 70-year-old Professor of Sociology at Georgetown University where he has taught since 1970 and continues to teach. These thoughts were provoked by recent reunions at St. John's Prep (Danvers, MA) and at Notre Dame.

Alexandre Papa—The One Thing We Know

Everything in life is uncertain. You never know who you'll bump into, where you'll end up by the end of the day, or even why that person you just passed by is sputtering incomprehensible nonsense. However, one thing that is always known for sure is that everybody's life will come to an end sooner or later. What will be going through my mind when that time comes for me?

People. People I have met. People I have associated with. People I have helped. People I have hurt. Have I made a difference in anybody's life?

Places. Places I have lived. Places I have visited. Places I have helped. Places I have ruined. Have I changed any places for the better?

Things. Things I have bought. Things I have borrowed. Things I have made. Things I have destroyed. Have I made anything worthwhile?

The only thing I know for certain is that there will be an end. I don't know why and I don't know how. But if I can answer yes to any of these questions, then I will be fulfilled.

Alex Papa is a 2013 graduate of the University of Rhode Island with a degree in Secondary Education and Spanish. Alex loves helping people, and is building on his nature to become the best Spanish teacher he can be. Alex also has a deep passion for capturing the world around him and recording his daily life with his camera. As an independent photographer, he has photographed various University events and worked with models, athletes, and performers. He is in the process of building up his own photography business.

Marc Tetreault—I Don't Think About Death

First of all I disagree with your premise unless you are only asking certain people for their opinions. It seems that this question can only apply to those who are obsessed with death, who can be considered older, or those who have just been told that they are terminally ill and have a limited number of days, weeks, even years left to live.

Having said that, I find meaning and fulfillment in my life despite the fact that I know " it ends in death" because I don't think about death. You may say that that makes me part of the control group and that I fall in the category of those who deny death—willfully put it out of their minds. So be it.

I can find meaning in my life because I consider death as part of life and that it will take care of itself and me when the time comes. For one thing I may not be there (consciously) when it happens as for example if I were to die in my sleep or if I were to lose my mind in dementia. When my spouse complains that life is too short and that what a bummer it is that it has to end in death I say to her that she should not be focusing on the last things but on the present. I like to think of life in a vertical way—the right now, the today, the experience I am having at this moment, and not horizontally with the end in sight. Perhaps I owe this to my mother who, quoting the bible, used to often say "sufficient unto the day is the evil thereof". That may indicate that I am a shallow person, not serious, just looking for a good time and that only serious persons can "handle the truth" and face up to the idea of death.

If you don't expect any more in life than the here and now, taking pleasure in what you are experiencing now, then your life can have meaning.

I have to admit that that way of thinking is prompted by the sense and knowledge that life is finite but you choose to ignore it. Make the most of it. Suck it up. Everyone dies at sometime or other.

Marc Tetreault is an artist but "Phil's the name and fun's my game" is a phrase I use more and more now that I am near 80 and retired. But it seems like I lived with that frame of reference ever since I escaped my mother's firm hand upon leaving for prep school. My wife is more of the mind that one can only espouse that way of being in the world if one is independently wealthy and has no sense of responsibility to society. Some of my friends think of me as "eccentric" where I would go more for "shallow" and that also helps explain my attitude toward death.

CHAPTER TWO

Death Does Not Obliterate Creativity But Intensifies It

"Don't let it end like this. Tell them I said something."
—Pancho Villa

Lisa Andrews—Creativity Triumphs Over Time

I imbue my life with meaning and joy by marveling at the diversity of life, celebrating the creative in and around us, and sharing love and faith with those whose paths cross mine.

Long influenced by the works of the French 20th century author and statesman, Andre Malraux, I find particularly profound the themes he examines in his paired works "La Condition Humaine" (transl. Man's Fate), and "L'Espoir" (transl. Man's Hope). In Man's Fate he considers the harsh and frustrating realities of mankind's inevitable struggle to survive among limited resources. In contrast, Man's Hope is devoted to the indomitable spirit of human creativity and the immeasurable power of artistic expression to influence, inspire and enhance every aspect of life.

"In a world in which everything is subject to the passing of time, art alone is both subject to time and yet victorious over it."—Malraux, 1975

What is certain in our lives? The need for sufficient air, water, food, clothing and shelter. Likewise we universally accept the scientific boundaries of the human life cycle: birth, growth, maturation and eventually certain death. We ARE all very much the same. Like many if not most, I've survived the death of loved ones; it is a sobering and life-altering experience. To me life is at its most interesting and satisfying when we take the time to discover, respect and celebrate our differences. This is indeed a challenging, creative and thrilling lifelong process.

Lisa Andrews is a married 60-year-old mother of two young adults, retired administrator for the State of Rhode Island, and devoted reader, sewist, fan of music and all things French. She was educated at the University of Rhode Island and SUNY at Stony Brook, NY with degrees in Psychology and Business Administration. She has lived her adult life along the shoreline in Saunderstown, Rhode Island, where she has been active volunteering in the local North Kingstown schools, and as a lifelong member of the Westminster Unitarian Church.

Russell R. Chabot—The Last Dance, the Last Laugh and to Hell with Socrates

I am sixty-years-old. How I got to live this long is a mystery perhaps not only to me, but also to many who have known me, particularly to those who knew me when I was much younger and more rambunctious. I guess it is called, "youthful risky behavior" today, no? I mention my age for a number of reasons. I lost my father when he was in his late sixties. Aside from the seven-years war between us, from when I was fourteen until I was about twenty-one years of age, we got along pretty well. The same goes for my mother, though I lost her in her mid-seventies. There was plenty of laughter and singing between them. As I approach their ages of departure, I start to hear the knock of mortality more clearly, everyday would be a dramatic overstatement, but it is there. How I came to know death is the subject of another essay.

The loudest knock I hear comes when I think of Karen, my late wife of almost twenty-one years, who saw me through many travails, especially through the last round-up that culminated in the completion of my Ph.D. dissertation. I dedicated it to her. I wrote, "To say that Karen is 'lively' doesn't do justice to all the ways that quality expresses itself in her," as she is "my companion, wife and fellow musical traveller."

So, how do I face the day knowing that the end will come for me as well. Simple, music and laughter. Yes, of course, I care about the world, and the dreadful state that it is in, but my parents, Roger and Ricky, conveyed that to me, before I knew of Kenneth Patchen's poetry and the spirit of, "Hallelujah anyway." Karen, oh what I would do for one more dance with you. And, one more time to send you laughing hysterically to the bathroom because you are on the verge of losing control. Oh how you amused me as well. Your last words ring in my head, "I know you love me, now get the hell out of here." There it is, or there they are, the music and laughter that allow me to face the knowledge of the inevitable. In the end, if there had been an opportunity to include photographs with this essay, I would have offered the following: Karen in her garden in a silly bird-like pose with the hose; Ma and Dad in a tight loving and laughing embrace; and two photographs from a recent trip to New Orleans, at a club, The Spotted Cat, of musicians and their audience so engaged with one another that audience/performer distinction disappears in the mutually reinforcing exuberance of the occasion. It is just this, all of this and what they embody that keeps me going from this day forward.

Russ Chabot grew up in Central Falls, RI. He earned a Ph.D. in sociology by studying local reggae bands. On Monday nights he can usually be found at Bovi's Tavern in East Providence where two of his interests come together: jazz and photography. This is the site of a 45-plus year big-band performance, and he has been photographing it for about three years (about 15,000 photographs up to now). He can also be found as a regular attendee of art openings and at the movies being shown at local art house cinemas. Otherwise, he is an associate professor of sociology at Johnson & Wales University.

Michael Geisser—Finding a Happy Place

I have found that true happiness, true fulfillment, is a balance between extremes: between obsessing and neglecting, wanting and needing, fighting and loving, narcissism and loss of self. For me, the search for happiness became necessary when I thought about the end, the specter of just disappearing. I had a hard time imagining nothingness; I needed to find comfort in spite of that reality. In my search, I have come to the conclusion that when I don't obsess about something, but give it what I consider to be its proper due, not neglect it, I am comfortable. When I reduce my wants to a minimum, to the point where fulfilling one of them is a special treat, not just scratching an itch, I am comfortable. When I try to understand the other, realize that this is not a perfect world, reduce my anger to a minimum, keep my place in society in perspective, I am comfortable. When I feel comfortable, feel nothing is out of sync with my world, I am happy.

From my happy place, I have looked at what I mean to myself, and the world as I see it, knowing my search would now encounter uncluttered paths. I have found that I want my efforts to bolster the main wave that carries what I believe in, not create a splash that mixes with the innumerable others that have no purpose or direction. That is the impact I want to leave to the world, to do with as it pleases.

Michael Frederick Geisser is a writer who has focused on parsing the meaning in and of his life since being diagnosed with a debilitating motor neuron disease ten years ago. Originally a student of philosophy and political theory, Mr. Geisser had almost finished a successful career in the field of hazardous waste engineering when the disease struck. Presently, he lives and writes in a cottage overlooking the Kickemuet River in Warren, RI, with his wife, Anna, and wonder dog, Kosmo.

Galen A. Johnson–Philosophy Matters to Me

By now, so many dead loves: parents gone, all the grandparents, classmates, friends. The sudden accidental death of a best friend in full life and health makes me dislike most the sudden shocking death and its roll of the dice.

Philosophy matters to me. "Where death is, I am not; where I am, death is not" (Epicurus). "Remember that you are an actor in a drama, of such a kind as the author pleases to make it. If short, of a short one; if long, of a long one" (Epictetus). My Christian father prayed at supper for the death of his cancer ravaged wife in her ninth day of coma, my mother, far too young, and the doctors turned up the morphine.

So among the contemporary philosophers, I distrust most those like Heidegger and Camus who speak of death as a friend because it lends urgency to living. The philosophers closest to my heart are those like Arendt and Merleau-Ponty who raise up natality above mortality and celebrate being-toward-birth rather than being-toward-death. New life and all the ages of life matter. These others matter.

So it was that the sudden death of a dear nephew last spring at age one and a half was inconsolable tragedy. The boy just didn't wake up from his nap. There were no words then, no philosophies, just hours on hours of holding hands and touching. And deep silence. "Time is the way offered to all that will be to be no longer. It is the invitation to die, for every phrase to decompose...addressed to the ear of *Sigé* the abyss" (Paul Claudel, *Sigé* = silence). I do still like the gospel hymns. Just the music, no words.

Galen A. Johnson is a professor of philosophy at the University of Rhode Island who specializes in the study of recent French philosophy, especially aesthetics. His most recent book is titled THE RETRIEVAL OF THE BEAUTIFUL. In relation to this work, he and his wife, Jean, enjoy traveling to see the art of the world and experience its food, people, and places. Together they are devoted to their six children, three grandchildren, old and new friends, and spend weekends enjoying the beaches of RI. Galen is also a lifelong cabinet maker specializing in furniture crafted from cherry and other local hardwoods

Jhumpa Lahiri—Life and Death in the Creative Process

In the summers I work in the studio of a painter who died a decade ago. I never knew him. Behind me are his easels, palette, cans of brushes and tools. I pace the same floor, contemplate the same sky he once did. He is everywhere and nowhere. He has become a companion, but remains a perfect stranger.

The painter's effects, stored in one corner, inspire me to work, while also reminding me that one day I will not. When I am writing I lose consciousness of time, but writing, here especially, reminds me that my hours are limited.

When I am at my happiest—when I am on Cape Cod, for example, working in this studio, I am intensely aware of life passing. I will swim in the ocean a certain number of days; I will share a meal with my husband at sunset a certain number of times. I will read stories aloud to my children a certain number of evenings, before they outgrow this ritual.

Though a fiction writer draws from life, either real or imagined, the act of writing is in some ways a simulation, perhaps an ongoing rehearsal, of death. Everyone enters and exits the world alone, but writers withdraw deliberately for long periods. I spend most of my days in solitude, disconnected, meditating on the impermanence of things.

The fulfillment of creative work is embedded in the here and now. Though I work slowly toward completion, it is the daily visitation that sustains me. Though the process takes place in a netherworld, I never feel as alive as when I am writing. Each day, when I stop, when I come up for air, I experience a brief death.

I will close with words of an Italian poet, Umberto Saba, that I discovered this morning before sitting down to work: *Ed e il pensiero della morte che, infine, aiuta vivere.* "And it's the thought of death that helps us, after all, to live."

Fiction author Jhumpa Lahiri was born in London and raised in Rhode Island. Her many awards and prizes include a Guggenheim Fellowship, the Pulitzer Prize, and the PEN/Hemingway Award. She lives in Brooklyn, New York with her husband and two children. She and her family are spending 2013-2014 in Rome where she is teaching, lecturing and writing. Her most recent novel is THE LOWLAND (Knopf, 2013).

Lynn Pasquerella–Mystic Unity and Baseball

As a philosopher, questions of life's meaning are central to my teaching and scholarship. While now a college president, I remember vividly the existential angst of my introductory philosophy students during our final section on death and the meaning of life. I began the discussion by asking them to tell me something—anything, really—about their maternal great-great grandmothers. Of the hundreds of students I taught over the years, not one could ever provide even a name. "So," I said, "here's a woman who is responsible for your very existence, and you cannot even tell me her name. What hope is there a hundred years from now that anyone will ever know you existed and, without that, can anything you do in life really matter?" It was a cruel question to ask, especially in the fall semester, when darkness descended early and the impending holidays incited their own anxieties.

Though I never revealed this to my students, for me, meaning and fulfillment come in two forms: service to others, and baseball. While it may not seem obvious to anyone else, I see an inextricable link. In the grand scheme of things, my life will not matter. Yet, the service I perform for others by promoting women's education and liberal learning, as a medical ethicist, and as a prisoner's rights advocate does matter to those whose lives are impacted. What provides meaning is akin to the Jewish immigrant experience with baseball in the early part of the twentieth century–an experience described by philosopher Morris Raphael Cohen as "redemption from the limitations of our petty lives," and a "mystic unity with a larger life of which we are a part." Baseball also offers what another philosopher of the sport, Bart Giamatti, unveils as the fostering and betrayal of the illusion that there is "something abiding, some pattern and some impulse that could come together to make a reality that would resist corrosion." In the process, baseball reminds us of "how slight and fragile are the circumstances that exalt one group of human beings over another." Whether I am in the stands at Fenway or in the broader community, on those darkest of days, and despite the inevitability of the game's end, I find meaning in that mystic unity with something larger than myself.

My fondest wish is that my students gained a similar fulfillment from the collective enterprise regarding life's meaning upon which we embarked.

Lynn Pasquerella is the president of Mount Holyoke College. A champion of women's education, the centrality of liberal learning, and access to higher education, she is the host of The Academic Minute, a public radio program introducing global listeners to cutting-edge issues in the academy. Her husband John, and their twin sons, Pierce and Spencer, share her love of baseball and are avid Red Sox fans.

Karen Stein—How to Live

Nature, poetry, music, and friendship are my guides to life. Rachel Carson wrote lyrically about the beauties of the ocean, and found that nature sustained her through difficult times. She wrote: "Those who dwell…among the beauties and mysteries of the earth are never alone or weary of life….Those who contemplate the beauty of the earth find reserves of strength that will endure as long as life lasts."

Singer and songwriter Phil Ochs expressed it so well I can't imagine saying it any better (the lines are his, but scrambled:)

"You won't find me singing on this song when I'm gone,
The pleasures of love will not be mine when I'm gone,
I won't breathe the bracing air when I'm gone,
I won't see the golden of the sun when I'm gone
All my days won't be dances of delight when I'm gone,
So I guess I'll have to do it when I'm here."

Karen F. Stein teaches English and Gender and Women's Studies at the University of Rhode Island. She has written books about three authors whom she admires: Margaret Atwood, Toni Morrison, and Rachel Carson. She is working on a book about American poet Adrienne Rich. Her passions are reading, walking, swimming, kayaking, and spending as much time in, on or near the water as possible.

CHAPTER THREE

Our Relationships Are More Important Than Our Mortality

"One day your life will flash before your eyes. Do your best every day to make sure its worth watching."
—Melchor Lim

Jack J. Barry, Jr.–Improving the Finite Human Condition

Here's hoping my Rock keeps rolling…. Honestly, I did not think seriously about death until I was in my early twenties. Camus argues that many live as if they are in denial of death and it seems that American society is especially egregious with regards to this denial. We are a country of opportunity, youth, optimism, and consumption, which often leads to convenient ignoring of death. Until I began to think about my inevitable death—unsettling as it seemed—I was solidly in the denial camp. At this formative time, I was exposed to existential philosophers, political theorists, and mentors who helped mold my own take on death, and surprisingly, towards finding meaning in my life.

Camus states: 'Crushing truths perish from being acknowledged.' The truth he is expounding on is our impending 'absurd' death. Once exposed, one is free to live life, despite knowing it may be absurd, and that we can enjoy living it. Camus' absurd hero, Sisyphus, is able to, so why can't I? Sisyphus's fate belongs to him, his Rock is his thing. Yet Camus and the existential philosophers left me ultimately frustrated by not providing many answers to what true meaning is in life. I found that by focusing on my own mortality, meaning in life became crystallized. Now in my early thirties, I think that loving and taking care of people, be they family, friends or even strangers, combined with giving back to my community, gives my life meaning even in the face of the annihilation that death brings. Improving the finite human condition, as long as I keep to as high a moral road as I possibly can, provides all the meaning I need. That high road takes many shapes, for me it is never treating people as commodities. I hope my Rock continues to roll down this high moral road despite the bumps, curves, eventual cliffs on the horizon. For me, my Rock keeps rolling to the beat of love in the face of death.

Jack J. Barry, Jr., age 33, grew up in Kingston, Rhode Island riding the local waves whenever they were large enough for surfing. As an East Coast surfer, he always kept a keen eye on weather systems, even considering being a meteorologist until he realized the only reason he was truly interested was to know when the fickle waves would be epic. Now he is pursuing his Ph.D. in Political Science from the University of Connecticut, yet he still manages to make time for surfing in his beloved Ocean State and playing pickup basketball.

Missy Buchanan—Leaning Forward Into Life

People often ask me how I keep from getting depressed. As an author, writer and speaker on issues of aging and faith, my days are filled with thoughts of growing old, death and dying. I was a caregiver for my own aging parents and I regularly visit older adults who are homebound or who live in care centers. People are surprised when I tell them that being surrounded by the aged is actually life-affirming for me. Through older adults I have learned not to sugar-coat the tough realities of aging but to embrace the mystery of the journey and the promise of eternity.

Typically I find that older folks are not afraid of death. It's that time between growing old and dying that concerns them most. They know that no one gets to the far end of life's timeline without having experienced great loss, including the death of friends and family and the loss of independence. At the same time, those who find new ways to serve others and to share wisdom through their life stories discover a renewed energy. I find purpose in walking alongside those who need a boost of encouragement. I remind them that they are not yet finished. They have opportunities to shape their legacy and to influence others as they lean forward into life, even as the finish line draws near.

Missy Buchanan is an author and speaker on issues of aging and faith. She has appeared twice on Good Morning America with Robin Roberts and co-authored MY STORY, MY SONG: MOTHER-DAUGHTER REFLECTIONS ON LIFE AND FAITH with Robin and her mother, Lucimarian Roberts. Missy is also the author of LIVING WITH PURPOSE IN A WORN-OUT BODY, JOY BOOSTERS and other titles for Upper Room Books. She travels worldwide to speak to retirement communities and church organizations. She resides in Rockwall, TX with her husband, Barry. www.missybuchanan.com

Russell Corcoran—The Privilege of Caring

The question I have been asked to answer has led me to think deeply over the past few weeks. "In the face of Death, how do you find meaning and fulfillment in life?" I am a internist, geriatrician, former hospice medical director, father, husband and son. These questions affect my daily life and I discuss them with my patients on a regular basis. This subject is not easy to approach because our society is a death denying society. If death is not mentioned it might not happen. The doctor- patient relationship I have had with my patients over many years has made these discussions easier.

So what have I learned with time and these discussions. The life we live is precious and we need to make the most of it. We can't put ourselves in other's shoes in making these tough decisions; some cling to life while others let it go peacefully. The things people value when faced with death are family, friends, memories and faith. The discussions that I have had with my patients have ranged from the physical to the metaphysical. I have had 90 year old patients tell me "Russell, don't get old", but they would not trade any of their time for a shorter stay here on earth despite their struggles.

So what will I do when faced with these challenges? I will be thankful that my wife, daughter and friends have taught me to live with vigor and enjoyment. I will be happy that I've had the privilege to care for people and make a difference in their lives. I will be glad that I spent time with my family, friends and patients. I will be glad that I have faith in God and that there is something to follow this life.

Russ Corcoran, MD, is an internist who has practiced geriatrics, medical acupuncture and general internal medicine in Wakefield, RI for the past 28 years. He is an avid Friar, Yankee and Patriot fan. His favorite pastimes are sailing with friends and family on Narragansett Bay and playing tennis.

Lu Cribari—Sweetness at the End

I am thinking about fine lines at the cosmetic counter at Nordstrom and eyeing the philosophy products with names that project powerful messages from Madison Avenue: Miracle Worker, Hope in a Jar and Eye Hope—marketing hype to soften confrontation with our own mortality. Even as I hand over my credit card, I chuckle at the puns I am buying into in the name of creature comfort.

It is something my late 93-year-old mother-in-law and I enjoyed together to the end. Might she have some lip balm, she asked one day from her hospital bed. My husband and I rushed to the local pharmacy and bought several, one in each flavor. She clutched the small gift after smearing her lips, which were dry from labored breathing. There is hope in comfort and comfort in hope.

On another day in a different hospital room, we spoke of things that make life good. It was nothing momentous but it took on great moment as that was to be her last day. She needed her New York Times, though she was too weak to read it. Holding the pages seemed to anchor her in a routine honed over a lifetime. I don't remember the headlines. Her thoughts shifted to lunch and the bland nourishment of the healthcare system: a restricted diet. Why she asked don't they put salt in the spinach? I had no answer and instead suggested she try the applesauce. She turned up her nose at my offering. It was unsweetened.

Lu Cribari is a writer, editor and blogger. A native of Colorado, and a resident of Rhode Island for many years, she now lives in New York City with her husband Dave Reid where they maintain a foodie perspective that life comes with healthy doses of salt and sugar. She worked as a journalist and community environmental activist but is most widely known as an expert fudge and brownie maker and pie baker. They have two amazing sons who urged her to start a brownie truck before it was the rage. She is learning to listen to her children.

Frank D'Andrea—Death, A New Adventure

On a recent trip to Greece I was on a completely full plane. Well into the flight the attendant broke the silence with unusual statements. "Is there anyone smoking? You are reminded it is illegal to smoke anywhere on the plane and you will be prosecuted to the full extent of the law." "Is anyone using an electronic device or forgot to turn off their computer? There should not be a computer or other electronic device being used."

Without word, the plane began to descend. In tense calm, we looked around at each other. Finally the captain announced because of mechanical problems we would be landing in Manchester, England. When we landed safely hundreds of emergency vehicles lined the runway, their lights directed into the landing space.

I knew I just lived through a serious life event. I wasn't afraid of dying but I found it to be very sobering. It was one of life's experiences that I identify as "it is what it is." There are situations that I have little or no control over, things that I do not have the power to change. I tell myself to deal with the situation the best I can and not to moan or complain why me, why now, this is unfair!

When I was young, about 6 years old, I would go by myself by bus to neighboring towns. I had a naive excitement in a new adventure. Somehow I knew I would find my way home. But soon life's disappointing and painful experiences changed excitement of new adventure to fear, pain and darkness.

About the sobering event, I realized I don't know if there is a supernatural being called God. When others talk about their god's approval or disapproval on human actions, I believe their god is too small. Their god is their own fabrication, made in their own image, limited by their capacity to think and feel. This god is as small as they are.

Death for me is what it is. I will not live my life in fear of death; in fear of a god interested in punishing us with an accounting of life lived or if there is no supernatural power to continue life after death. I decided to look on death as a new adventure, and to recapture some of my childhood naive excitement about beginning an adventure into the unknown. Besides if death just ends life, I will not have the painful consciousness to feel and know that my life is over and ended anyway.

At age 69, Frank D'Andrea is living with Parkinson's disease. Frank has the good luck to be able to travel frequently. For the past 8 years he has made one or two visits to Greece each year, a month and a half each time. What luck. His motto is: "Life is what it is and be grateful for what it is."

Shawnee M. Daniels-Sykes—Meaning in Life: A Brother's Struggles

On August 14, 1970, my mother told my five siblings and me that she needed to go to the hospital; she would be having her seventh baby. I was 10 years old. Later on that evening, my dad came home only to tell us that the baby boy, Stewart Sykes, was very sick and not expected to live very long. Years later (after majoring in biology and nursing in college), I recalled my mother's narrative around Stewart's birth, life, and death; I realized what the problem was. During my mother's early stages of the pregnancy ammonium fumes escaped into the air in a factory where my mother worked. Stewart had severe congenital neurological and respiratory problems. His left lung had not developed, he did not have a cough reflex, he was a quadriplegic. Most notably, during his twenty-two months of life, Stewart was in an out of the hospital. I watched my parents faithfully address his urgent healthcare needs. I was deeply affected by this deep desire for Stewart to have a quality life. He died on June 9, 1972.

At the age of 11, I knew that I would find meaning and fulfillment in life as a result of Stewart's health struggles and death. Today, I am the only Black Catholic female bioethicist in the United States. Among other areas, I have dedicated my life towards helping others even in the face of imminent death.

Sr. Shawnee M. Daniels-Sykes is a 52-year-old professor and Director of the Honors Program at Mount Mary College. She has been auto-immune suppressed for many years to mitigate the traumatic effects of Crohn's Disease. She is passionate about addressing issues that adversely impact human dignity and flourishing. During her spare time, she enjoys weightlifting, tread milling, and swimming. Most recently, she has been taking photographs of the death shrines erected in the city of Milwaukee as a result of violent gun homicides.

Joshua Feinman—All that Really Matters Are Your Relationships

"In the face of death, how do you find meaning and fulfillment in life?"

I have spent some very late nights and early mornings cursing the two of you for this opportunity.

"The meaning of Life…?"

After my father's death on 12/15/10, meaning and fulfillment in life were difficult concepts to comprehend. Shock, sadness, loneliness and fear were much easier.

The Big Question….

What will we do now?

The empty space in our hearts only he has filled.

My father loved life. He knew its meaning.

"Dad, how did you find meaning and fulfillment in life after your father, mother and brother passed?"

He could always get me to think.

Dad was a student of life, he found fulfillment in reading and learning and listening. Loved to discuss what he learned. He loved his family and friends. Made sure we knew it. We loved him too. We still do.

On 1/11/11 my daughter, his first grandchild was born.

27 days to grieve? I don't think I did it right.

I am still sad for a part of everyday.

My daughter deserves to be happy. So do my wife, mother, sister, and even me. Dad would want us to be happy and live life. As if he were still here.

When I made him proud. That's when I felt my best.

Raise my daughter as he raised me.

Listen to her as he always listened to me.

Contribute to society and your daughter will follow in your footsteps. And so will her children.

There is no greater meaning or purpose in life then to give back.

Fulfillment will be watching her grow up.

All that really matters in life are your relationships. And after life, all that matters is the legacy you leave behind.

Meaning and fulfillment in life come as you shape your legacy. My father's legacy will live for a very long time. He made a difference in this world. I will do the same. And that is how I will find meaning and fulfillment in life in the face of death.

Josh Feinman is an actor and producer born and raised in the Bronx, and currently residing in Los Angeles. He now works in film, television and on stage. Most recently Josh has produced, co-written, co-directed and acted in the award winning series FRONT SEAT CHRONICLES (FSC). FSC is a current web-series in its third season and deals with many of life's most challenging issues. Josh loves the Yankees, surfing, playing basketball and most of all his beautiful wife and daughter.

Timothy Heffernan–Weaving the Tapestries of Family and Community

L ife is lived in the contrasts of our experiences. Our experiences are the images, our reactions are our choice of color, and the purpose we place on the meaning form the brush strokes that paint our personal tapestries.

A birth, a first kiss, getting into a University, winning a race, laughing with friends, weddings, reunions, deaths, they all evoke an emotion that contrasts the experience that emit a different color unique to individuals in life. Placing purpose on the contrasts define meaning and fulfillment of intrinsic goals where individuals find happiness.

It is hard to find the meaning and fulfillment because we remove the certain uncertainty of death with religion as our first mechanism to deal with the contrast of despair. Despair rips at the fabric of what makes the human experience fulfilling because it tears at meaning and purpose.

Religious dogma reinforces the removal of contrast. It creates a paint-by-the numbers guide to the answers on the images of life. The result is a clear picture, but ultimately an unsatisfying one because it was defined by someone else. With no pride in ownership, meaning is lost and the art is not worth viewing once completed.

We look to automate our lives and remove contrasts to whitewash suffering. We follow the same path to work, stitch together the same routine and neutralize experiences through routine. Assigning purpose is hard. It takes self-awareness to place a purpose between stimulus and response to create our own quilts.

Weaving our tapestries together form the quilts of families, communities, countries and society. Depending on how much and what we weave leaves behind a guide to legacy, learning and love for future weavers.

Tim Heffernan (@nycheff) is a thinker who turns ideas into actions in the areas of business, technology and politics. After leading government relations, emerging businesses and communications functions within Fortune 500s, he co-founded Aperio Strategy, a corporate development firm. Heffernan holds a Bachelor of Arts degree in political science from the University of Rhode Island. He resides in Babylon, NY with his wife, Abigail.

Paul Kile—Walking Among the Trees

After walking among the mighty redwoods as a young man, I was taken by their longevity and beauty. They brought awareness that without trees our planet will have no life. Jared Diamond's work Collapse (Diamond, Jared M., <u>Collapse: How Societies Choose to Fail or Succeed</u>. Penguin Group Inc., 2005), provides strong evidence that our trees are our lifeline. Most of my life I have been planting trees as I move around the country. I visit some of them via Google Earth to see how they are doing.

My present meaningful project is the development of a polyculture (Shepard, Mark, <u>Restoration Agriculture, Real-World Permaculture for Farmers</u>. ACRES U.S.A. Austin, Texas, 2013) of food bearing trees in an extreme northern climate that can live for centuries once established. J. Russell Smith (Smith, J. Russell, <u>Tree Crops, A Permanent Agriculture</u>. New York, Harcourt, Brace and Company, 1950) noted chestnut groves in Corsica that were grafted in Roman times. I expect many of the trees I plant to begin reaching maturity long after I am gone, providing food, wood, jobs for the local community, oxygen, protecting soil, water, and wildlife habitat.

It gives me peace and purpose to envision walking among these old friends as I age, and ultimately my ashes scattered among them to be absorbed in an almost animistic way.

As a physician I confront death daily in the lives of my dying patients. This has kept ever present the fact that my heart too will stop beating in a matter of time, short or long. My greatest fulfillment in life has been raising my sons with my wife to be productive members of society with strong family values.

Paul Kile was born in 1950 in North Dakota near Lemmon, South Dakota where his grandparents homesteaded in the late 1800's, living in a sod hut on the prairie. He grew up in the Black Hills of South Dakota 200 miles south of there, frequenting the logging camps with his father. Their lives were centered around trees. He served as a hospital corpsman in the Navy during Vietnam, became a Licensed Practical Nurse, and went to medical school, finishing up in Boston at Beth Israel Deaconess. He stayed on the east coast and never lost his love for trees.

John Killilea—Life, Love, Motivation

The one certain reality in life is that it will have an end. Death is a certainty for everyone. None of us escapes. This being the case, what gets me going and keeps me on the path to life's completion? The priorities change with each new life stage but the motive remains steady…love, in marriage, in raising a family, in challenging self and finding fulfillment in one's life tasks. Now in the eighth decade of my life, I keep going. Why?

I'm still motivated by love, care for my wife particularly, and enjoyment of my family generally.

Self-fulfillment is another motivator. Whether it is learning a second language or doing something I have wanted to do, the satisfaction is there and I find it's worth working for.

Another motivating factor for me is leaving this world a little better because I spent some time here. This involves working with others for a cause that affects the lives of people for the better. Seeing people better themselves because of some effort where I have played a part is its own reward.

Yes, death is a certainty, and it's going to happen to me sometime. I just want to live life fully until that fateful hour.

This essay does not treat of the meaning of death, which is another topic in itself. However, I do believe that one's understanding of death does affect one's motivation in living.

An avid reader and sometimes a writer, John Killilea resides in South Carolina. His interests include politics, history, psychology, theology, advances in science and anything else that stimulates thinking and conversation. John and his wife, Aida, lived for four years in Mexico where he was able to mix with local people and expats in Guadalajara. In addition to some volunteer work, John enjoys keeping up with his kids and grandkids.

Jane McCarthy—Seek Peace with Your Adversaries

We know for certain that the sun sets every day. Sometimes it is bright and you can see it set. At other times, it is obscured by clouds and fog. But surely it will set. Life is like the sun, it will go on in the face of adversity, success, failure, happiness and loss.

To find meaning in the face of death, make your life matter. Matter to those whom you care about and even those you do not. Seek peace with your adversaries. Put yourself into your feelings, your beliefs and your work. Show your love to those around you. Rejoice in the accomplishments of others. Seek beauty and goodness in others.

To find fulfillment in the face of death, blow the sawdust out of your head. Be authentic in what you say or do. Be open to others who do not share your ideals and who differ with your ideas. Contribute to the wellbeing of others. Extend a hand. Say a prayer.

A 96-year old woman was asked if she wanted to prolong her life or let death come naturally. Her answer: "I've done everything I wanted to do."

Death will surely come. Some of us will have time to find meaning and fulfillment in life. Others may not. Give yourself time while you can. Make a list. It will be easier when the sun sets on you.

Jane F. McCarthy has a fulfilling career as a registered nurse and has a fulfilling marriage to Gerry for 50 years. They have three daughters and seven grandchildren.. She has traveled extensively with Gerry. One of her favorite memories is waking up in Morocco to the call to prayer with the scent of jasmine wafting through the open window. Jane is working on her first novel and is a member of a writing group that produces an anthology of their essays and poems annually.

W. Lynn McKinney—It's What You Don't Do That Matters

R as in a car accident at 23; Kyle of testicular cancer when 29; Richard of a heart attack at age 39; Tom of melanoma when 49. All age mates and best friends in their day. And that is not to begin to acknowledge those with HIV/AIDS or first cousins with cancer. I realized early on and had to acknowledge regularly thereafter that no days were guaranteed.

In an iconic Peanuts cartoon Charlie Brown realizes that the test of life is neither true/false nor multiple choice but a 1,000 word essay. I feel fortunate to have been able to write my own essay. Now, at age 70, I believe that Billy Crystal was wrong. It's neither how you feel nor how you look but what you do.

"You can't live a perfect day without doing something for someone who will never be able to repay you," is my favorite quotation from John Wooden. He also admonishes us to be more concerned with our character than with our reputation. "Character is who we are; reputation is who others think we are."

So I try to plan my days, weeks and months to focus on strengthening our communities and the lives of people in them and on being a devoted family member. I strive to be a good mentor to young gay men confronting coming out and other issues. I will continue to be active and supportive in organizations serving the particular needs of women. Not everyone has had the same opportunities that I had; I believe in enhancing human potential.

W. Lynn McKinney, Ph.D., University of Rhode Island retired dean and professor climbs aboard airplanes destined for other countries as frequently as possible. He also works to ensure quality programs in higher education through service to accreditation boards. He continues his commitment to local nonprofit organizations by service on the boards of the Domestic Violence Resource Center of South County and the Gamm Theatre.

Roberta Richman—The Answer to Mortality Is Kindness

In the face of death, how does one find meaning and fulfillment in life? A subject I dwell on often; one that intersects and overlaps with my feelings about religion, both organized and personal. Mortality is a lot easier to contemplate I think, when you have at least some glimmer of faith that there is more to one's life than the here and now. If life on some other level after death has ever crossed your mind as possible, you can I suppose, take some comfort at the thought that it might be. That doesn't work for me.

For me there is no falling back on the thought that death is anything other than final. I've never harbored the illusion that something else, something better, comes after death. As a young adolescent I recall thinking that people who really believe that there is a God—who never question that some great power controls our lives, are lucky. People of faith may be motivated to behave well because they believe they would be punished if they sinned. I never believed that. So why do I not sin? Why do I choose to love and forgive, to be kind, to give what I can to others? Is that what living a moral life means?

My acts of kindness give me a feeling of purpose and fulfillment. They are the greatest source of my joy. I have been fortunate to work in a world, a prison, where I can do small simple things to bring happiness to others. I can reach young men and women who have experienced little but pain during their lives, and give them encouragement and opportunities they ironically, would never have had if they had not been incarcerated. Their appreciation for small bits of attention and a chance to learn have been a source of meaning and purpose for over three decades of my life.

I learned late in life how important it is to reach out quietly to friends and family who are suffering pain or loss and that doing so fulfills me in a way I did not understand when I was younger. More important than seeking my own pleasure, it is another way I find meaning and a sense of purpose for my life.

As I age and my friends age with me, death is often on my mind. I've already outlived my parents and grandparents and am very aware of how fragile life is. My father was told he had six months to live and I lived those months with him in awe of how he went about saying goodbye to all he knew and loved. I wonder how I would feel, what I would do and say to my family and friends were it I who had received that news. I'd like to think I'll be at peace with my fate but am not sure that I will have the strength and courage that will require. I try to lead a mindful life, to get pleasure from the beauty of the world around me. I make the effort every day, to be mindful of my actions and thoughts. I try to listen and connect with the world and the people around me. I often fail but when I succeed, I'm conscious of living a meaningful life even in the face of my mortality.

Roberta Richman is an almost 73-year-old partner, mother and grandmother, artist, gardener, fledgling amateur musician, retired prison warden and Director of Rehabilitation for the RI Department of Corrections, and advocate for prison reform. She is committed to her partner, family and friends, to volunteer work for the Institute for the Study and Practice of Nonviolence where she is a member of the Board of Directors, to her art and to Hera Gallery as a founding member and member of the Board since its inception almost 40 years ago.

David Schock—If Love Is Real
Then Death Is Nothing

Death is something we tend to see as occurring for us in the future. Yet really it is always happening. Each day we age, and there is change in our life situation as well. Friends come and go, school, work, home life changes, and all are deaths of a kind.

The body apparently replaces all its cells every seven years—like the farmer who has had the same ax for 30 years, replacing the handle six times and the blade twice. Is it the same ax? And are we the same body? For it is primarily our body's "final" death we speak of as "death". Yet is this an illusion? We see our "death" in the future, yet science tells us time is not linear, but a product of the biological perspective of the body. What, then, is really happening? Perhaps a play of consciousness.

For me, I believe death is unreal. We are spiritual beings that inhabit a body for a while, and the passing of that body has no more effect on our "reality" than a change in attention and focus of our consciousness. This change tends to break communication, but this is not necessarily the case, as many have experienced connection with "passed" loved ones. Love is the power that bridges the worlds of life and death, as it empowers all things.

We live in a world in which all things seem to die, but perhaps none really do—only the changing form that we are choosing to see as loss, and in doing so perpetuate an illusion that serves other goals than love. If only love is real, the one creative force, then death is nothing. This is what the great masters have all taught, famous and not, great and small.

Dave Schock is an artist and spiritual teacher by trade. He lives in Wakefield, RI, with his family, and exhibits his paintings in galleries in New England and London. He is a trained teacher in yoga, Course in Miracles, Reiki and other stuff, too. Occasionally he plays basketball, and likes to shoot. He believes that only Love is Real, or at the very least believes that seems like the best option, and is trying to live this.

Peter W. Stein—Appreciating Miracles in Every Day

One of my colleagues and friends, a young man in his forties, passed away suddenly from an embolism. Shortly afterwards, I was attending a convention and witnessed a young man, also in his forties, collapse and die from a heart attack. That same week, back home, another young man, father to a boy at my son's elementary school, also passed away from a heart attack.

These events certainly gave me pause to reflect, in the face of death, on the fragility of life.

I find meaning in my own life in two related facts: no one lives forever and our lives can be remembered long after we die. We must take full advantage of each day that we have. There will always be more to do, whether we live to 100 in good health or whether circumstances cause us to die at a younger age.

The Jewish liturgy includes a series of blessings as part of the daily prayers. Each morning, we are to say a series of blessings about the "miracles in every day." The prayers urge us to see each day as an opportunity to do good, to take note each day of what is beautiful, and to cultivate an attitude of thankfulness for each day that we are alive. The blessings remind us that our bodies are fragile but our souls are eternal. This gives meaning to my days, as I try and make a difference, acting with love and working for the cause of peace and justice, praying that I will be remembered in some way after I am gone.

Rabbi Peter W. Stein serves as the spiritual leader of Temple Sinai in Cranston, Rhode Island. He is the president of the Rhode Island Board of Rabbis and past president of the Cranston Clergy Association. He has a particular interest in interfaith relations and creating opportunities for Catholic-Jewish dialogue and other inter-religious programming. Rabbi Stein was born and raised in New York, and is married with two children. He loves playing tennis, following the Red Sox, and playing and listening to music of all kinds.

John A. Sullivan—Life As a Cooperative Occupation

I've just turned seventy. I'm in fairly good health, but I'm decaying. Each day my body tells me it is a little less willing to do what it did yesterday, and my mind is a little less able to retrieve the name of that person I wanted to tell my wife about.

Now in retirement, I've found mentoring and tutoring young people very fulfilling. I don't preach or lecture, but if someone asks for help, I can be there and do the best I can.

As to the meaning of life, I don't believe in God or life after death. I don't belong to a religion, so I don't have any pre-established structure for the meaning or fulfillment of life. I have a strong sense of right and wrong, based on how much good or harm we do to others and to ourselves. We should try to make life as comfortable and agreeable as possible for ourselves and those we encounter along the way. I don't see life as a competition in which the one with the most toys is the winner. Life needs to be a cooperative occupation where our own self-concern doesn't overwhelm our concern for others.

I find life now not as intense, and while still trying to help others, I'm trying to enjoy as much as possible the time I have left.

John A. Sullivan has been retired for 15 years after working as an insurance executive for the same company for 33 years. He takes pride in the fact that during his career he was able to work with a wide variety of individuals (peers, subordinates and superiors) and always deal with them as ethical teammates in pursuit of the good of the company and its clients. He has a wonderful wife and daughter, and hopes to continue to enjoy life for some time to come.

Terry Thoelke—Always Be Kinder Than Necessary

Answering a student's question about God and Death, Confucius replied "That's God's business. Your business on Earth is helping your fellow man."

My purpose is clear—staying busy in helping my fellow beings, whether human or animal.

Without compensation, I open my tiny home to acquaintances and friends with no roof over their heads as they suffer hardships transitioning from home to home. Some stayed a few months, living in humble dignity, camaraderie and safety. Why let that tiny bedroom go unused? It is a useful space to someone.

"Always be kinder than necessary." I walk lost travelers to their destinations, and mothers with infants let me unload their cumbersome strollers from buses. Elders ask the least, but welcome assistance most graciously.

One day riding the bus I questioned my purpose—is it enough to simply be kind to others? At that moment of heightened self-doubt, a gentleman next to me said "I know you from the Bellevue grocery store. I'm the butcher—you never buy meat, but you always stop to chat with me. Thanks for that!" I had my answer.

Sir Walter Scott asked "Is death the last sleep? No, it's the final awakening," a positive statement about Death. We fear what we will experience when others die. Life is what terrifies us at that point, not Death.

My death will come. If it's truly the final awakening, I hope God evaluates whatever kindnesses I have given and received, deciding "Good job. I've another for you…"

Terry Thoelke is deaf and holds several degrees that have never been used in any of her unusual careers. A heightened curiosity about life styles and people in these great United States keeps her restlessly moving from state to state every few years, including a move from the smallest state, Rhode Island, to the biggest state, Alaska, where she married a Sourdough who is now studying for his Ph.D. in gerontology. She lives in the Midwest (for now) and has five books "in the works."

Barbara Tilden–The Consolation of Children and Kindness

D r. Bernie Siegel wrote "Do not spend time and energy trying to avoid dying-it is inevitable for us all." He was not saying we should just give up, he was explaining that our energy should be used in a positive way to enjoy each day. My husband is a glass half empty kind of guy and says we begin to die the day we are born. I guess in the literal sense, that is true but there is more to it.

I am a registered nurse and have had the opportunity to be with a great many people and their families as they have died. Some deaths are those you wish for—peaceful and blessed—and others are not. I have had the privilege to care for patients and family members who have come to the end of their lives. I have had the honor to sit with family members as they have said their last goodbyes to loved ones.

I am very lucky to have children and grandchildren who will carry some of me with them and hopefully pass along to other generations. It gives my life meaning to know how my children have grown and the men they have become. They embody the values I hold as important in a husband, father and man. The other way I find fulfillment is in my work. I know that a visit, having a kind word, holding a hand, rubbing a back, listening to fears, reading or just sitting quietly is very important to someone in need of comforting. I can do this and I think I am good at it. That gives me meaning and fulfillment.

Barbara Tilden, RN, is a clinical professional development manager at South Shore Hospital (Weymouth, MA) where she has practiced for many years. She is particularly interested in the area of access to health care. Barbara is married with two sons. She has two grandsons and three granddaughters.

Mark R. Tucker, III—A Secret Smile Gives Me Hope

In the face of death, how does one find meaning and fulfillment in life? The way the question is asked certainly puts death front and center. I think the real thrust, however, is "How and why do I continue to work, give birthday gifts and otherwise celebrate the milestones of life in the face of death?"

Dealing with death is a fact that not even politicians can spin to avoid it. You must deal with it. Death holds no sting for me as it is part of life. My closest contact with death has been through suicide. I have lived through several deaths by suicide. Suicide is the most selfish thing anyone can do. It robs the people left behind of so much and leaves them feeling guilty as well as bereaved. Even in the face of these deaths, including knowing that mine will eventually come, I still go to work. I am still poor. I still have bad health care and bad teeth. I know that I can't afford to change any of that and yet I still try to find something hopeful in life. I like that life's amazing, that it can be sad, that it is fascinating, sometimes surprising and always interesting. Life always engages my heart and mind because it affords me the garden, the younger generation, politics, art, history and the foibles of humanity around the world. Life, including my own, can be contradictory. I rant about suicide, but I still smoke like a chimney.

Life gives me the opportunity to learn and the more I learn, the more I can share with others even if only at times through that secret little smile that communicates a lot without the need for words. Christians call it the holy spirit. I call it being in touch with a part of the world.

It is those shared moments of understanding that give me hope and enjoyment in a life facing inevitable death.

Mark Tucker is a South Kingstown, RI native who was raised Roman Catholic and later sought religious direction with Episcopalians and Baptists. Although deeply spiritual, he has not had any formal religious affiliation since early adulthood. He is a bagel baker and also owns a floral design business. He enjoys travelling, and finds particular pleasure in cooking meals for friends and family.

Cynthia Weisbord—We Defy Death by Love

Any meditation on death is in its essence a contemplation of life, for death's reality or meaning exists only within the context of life. For there is no death in the absence of life. The experiences of my earliest years had not exposed me to the deaths of loved ones. When, at the age of eight I lost my mother, I had no grasp of its simplest and most profound meanings. I was not precocious enough to begin to understand the meaning of life, of its endless pieces and parts, large and small—most of all its final piece—death.

I have come now to believe that life has only that meaning we confer upon it. That being so, inevitable death, surrounding the mosaic of life, has only that meaning which each of us during our lifetime has come to discover.

How I envy those fortunate enough to have been taught, or to have concluded from their life experiences, that death brings them to happiness, brings them in fact not to a conclusion, but to a new beginning. As I'm not among those blessed with this belief, I must find the meaning of death in life. And in fact, I do. As life offers us much that is beautiful, creations of nature and of humans, perhaps its greatest gift is that of love. We can love in countless ways. Perhaps most powerfully we can reach out to touch another human's soul. It's in this gift of love that we have the opportunity to defy death.

Although I can't use John Donne's words, "One short sleep past, we wake eternally," I can take from him others and say "Death be not proud." Immortalized by the love we may show others, some unknown and half the earth away, and others whom we have wrapped in our arms, I can say "Death shall be no more. Death, thou shalt die. "

Cynthia Weisbord is a wife, mother and grandmother who taught school for many years. She was drawn to teaching as the most obvious and available way to engage in stretching the minds of children and adults. Many years later, amazed and fascinated during a walk on the jammed streets of Alexandria, Egypt, Cynthia studied the dynamics and impact of population growth and subsequently worked as the Education Coordinator of Planned Parenthood of Rhode Island. Although she claims no serious previous attempts at writing, she welcomed the opportunity to write about death. Because of her years, she felt that death by virtue of its approaching status, seems to welcome a consideration.

Reiko Wimbush–Laughter Heals a Cracked Heart

On facing my own departure, some thoughts enter my mind: "Did I live happily?" "Did I love fully?" It's hard to measure our own "fulfillment" because our expectations change as we move on in our lives, but happiness is simpler to measure. Happiness brings a burst of light: laughter. Family and friends laugh when I am happy. Love may be harder to measure—did he say "I love you last Tuesday?"—to measure, but laughter can be heard even from the next room! The cracking sound of laughter heals a cracked heart. Living is hard. We make many mistakes in our long lives even when our intentions are good. Do we ever need humor (laughter)! Laughter is an instinctive reaction of happiness…it's audio sunlight! It warms people's hearts. It cleanses us and we can love more and more. Laughter is an ambassador for peace. If my life were as positive as laughter, how happy I would be to know that I had brought a piece of peace in this otherwise hard world.

Reiko Wimbush is from Japan. She laughed so much in the convent in Kyoto, she was kicked out and landed in the USA 45 years ago. Her sense of humor brings happiness to her large circle of friends. She is an oil painter who exhibits at various venues. Her art history class at South Kingstown Senior Center attracts many people (latecomers are sometimes turned away) because they enjoy her lively style of teaching.

Morgan Zubof—The Lives We Have Touched

After losing my grandfather and aunt in a matter of only nine months I was forced to face a question that so many have faced before. How do we find meaning in life when our time is so uncertain? When it can end so much sooner than expected? The saying "to live each day like it's your last" simply seems insufficient. While it is true that the meaning of life cannot be found in the time we are given, but rather is defined by what we do with the time that is given to us, the meaning of life is far more complex than the saying would have us believe. The meaning of life can be found in our passions and in our fears, in our laughs and in our tears, in our words and in our deeds. The purpose of life is not only to live for oneself, but to live for the pursuit of something larger than oneself—to fight injustice, defend the weak, or love a child. At the end of our days, whenever it may come, a successful life is not measured by the balance in our bank account or the size of our home. Instead, success is measured by the number of people whose lives we have touched, the number of people who say that their lives have changed for the good because of us.

Morgan Zubof graduated from The George Washington University in 2008 with a BA in International Relations and she received her MA in Political Science at the University of Rhode Island in May 2013. Before moving to Rhode Island with her husband, Morgan worked at the Department of Defense as an intelligence analyst. She is currently filling her time with numerous hobbies, including improving her baking skills, playing with her dog, and learning to garden, as well as preparing for the arrival of her and her husband's first child.

CHAPTER FOUR

Views On The Necessity Of Faith

"To every thing there is a season, a time
to be born and a time to die."
—Ecclesiastes 3:1

William Bartels—Faith Imbues My Life with Meaning

I understand the assumption behind the question. If life is the improbable and accidental result of blind processes, if we are as insignificant in the universe as we are an infinitesimally small part of it, if each life is a mere spark that burns for the blink of an eye only to be extinguished forever, then how is any meaning possible at all? Indeed, it was this apparent absurdity that led Albert Camus to say that the only serious philosophical question was that of suicide.

But the question is framed personally, so my response reverses the order. It is not a question of how in the face of death I find meaning in life. Rather, it is because I have found meaning and fulfillment in life, that I can face death serenely. I was raised in a family that believed the universe was nestled in the embrace of a gracious and loving God. This belief, affirmed in my family, confirmed repeatedly in my experience, imbues my life with meaning. It also provides a purpose for my life perhaps best summarized in the Golden Rule and in the words of the ancient prophet, "...to do justice, to love kindness, and to walk humbly with your God." If I can reach the end of my life having lived accordingly then I will face death feeling I have left the world a bit better off than it was when I entered it. And that will be fulfillment enough.

William Bartels is Lecturer in Philosophy and Religious Studies at the University of Rhode Island where he also served as a Protestant chaplain. He received his Ph.D. in Religious Studies from Rice University, and has been teaching at URI since 1988. His areas of focus are world religions, ethics, and religious epistemology.

Michele Bronda—Death Does Not Belong to Us

All my life I have been working without ever thinking that someday I would have to address this issue. Death does not belong to us, it will never touch me and it is something of which most us do not ever think.

But time passes and then comes the moment of the accounting of our existence.

I am in this stage: I am 75 years old. Death has begun to make appearances in my life like when I had to watch the end of my parents, then of my dear friends. Seeing a parent or a friend die is to see a piece of your life die: everything you thought you knew changes, your landmarks disappear and you are increasingly alone.

This is the time to look back and to assess the life journey you have made. The difficult times of my past life are blurred by the fog of memory and have almost vanished. Now I think about my family: my wife (forty years together), our children and grandchildren and how they live their lives in harmony with the world. I think thankfully how I have more friends than enemies.

I begin to think about my work and gratefully one day a man with white hair reminds me that he was one of my students so long ago and says he did learn from my teaching. This makes me proud and I think I have done my duty.

I'd like to say: "Ego Me Absolvo", but unfortunately I cannot say it.

But, now that I'm approaching the big step I hope that the Divine Judge will forgive me my many sins which—deliberately—I do not remember.

His love for art led Michele Bronda to his position as a professor of art. He taught sculpture for almost thirty years at the oldest art school in Rome. His passion for art was fueled by the many wonderful paintings in his boyhood home by a famous uncle, Alessandro Mastro-Valerio. Now retired, the 75-year-old Bronda finds himself occupied with the restoration of paintings and writing. He recently published, in Italy, a well-received biography of his famous uncle. He and his wife have been married for many years and they occupy what free time they can find with children and grandchildren.

Nan Burke—An Experience of Dying

I was raised in the Catholic tradition. From a perspective infused by guilt and expected sacrifice and suffering, I always feared death. Three years ago, at the age of sixty-six, as I was falling asleep one night, I had a life-altering experience. I felt myself drawn into a gentle vortex of soft white light and wanted nothing more than to follow it. I felt myself swathed and cradled within the most exquisitely comforting, totally unconditional, non-judgmental love. Every cell of my body felt accepted and cherished; every fiber of my soul recognized itself in this Love. I wanted to follow deeper into this loving, body and soul embrace, but I sensed that there was no returning, so I literally had to force myself to open my eyes and to stop this deepening and blending.

I lay there in the familiar darkness of my room, soothed by a knowing that I was no longer afraid to die. In a way, I actually looked forward to it as a passage back into this sublime wholeness, this suffusion of love that I had just unexpectedly experienced.

The next morning, when I told my daughter, she suggested I had sleep apnea and agitatedly insisted that I get it checked. The next week I was tested overnight in a clinic and was told I had a calm, deep sleep pattern and was in a completely non-risk category.

I am filled with gratitude for this grace-infused experience. Three years later, I continue to live each day with this body-mind-soul remembering that I am loved. It is a knowing that not only am I loved unconditionally, but that I AM that love; I know that God and I are one and the same. When I die, I pass from this ever-changing physical body, but eternally remain Love and loved.

Born in New York City, and currently residing in Rhode Island, Nan Burke refers to herself as a human being, sharing lovely planet Earth in oneness with all creation. She has been a nun and bartender, a leader of SCUBA expeditions and manager of a B&B, a homesteader and trainer of parrots, a teacher and mother and grandmother, pretty much in that order but not necessarily those pairings! Nan is fortunate to have traveled the world, but has lived mostly on Long Island and in Puerto Rico. She has no regrets, considers nothing ever to have been a mistake, and urges everyone to follow one's heart, and live by the Golden Rule.

Michael A. Cerbo II—Death as Preparation in the Catholic View

Death is a subject that no one seems comfortable with. People like to have a sense of control, but death lets us all realize that ultimate control is out of our grasp. The death of a loved one can be a jarring experience of sorrow, fear and disappointment. No one is spared from these feelings when someone close to us passes. But for Catholics, we understand that these feelings will be replaced with joy and happiness. Death is where new eternal life begins. Admittedly, there are many clichés out there that everyone's heard but the power of faith to sustain those that are facing death, or those that have lost a loved one is incomprehensible. It is this belief in God during our lives that will sustain us at the end.

The Church gives us the means and direction to achieve that eternal hope. This life is not meant to be a utopia, and the pain and suffering of this world, even unto death, is a clear reminder that there must be something better waiting for us. There will always be anxiety, but hopefully those feelings will drive us to be the person that God has called us to be so that as President Reagan stated "...we will slip the surly bonds of earth to touch the face of God." (Reagan's Space Shuttle Challenger Tragedy Address, Jan 28, 1986).

Michael A. Cerbo II is a member of the faculty at the University of Rhode Island. He is responsible for maintaining the library's collection of e-resources and catalogs various library materials while serving as the Head of Copy Cataloging. Cerbo is a member of a local Catholic parish and serves on its council. He is married and has a daughter.

Judith V. Daley—Ready To Meet My Maker

At this point, I feel I am pretty organized in most aspects of life and I am ready to meet my Maker. I think I have done my best to live a life of which God will approve and that He will judge me accordingly. I believe in heaven and would be so happy to know that I will see loved ones who have passed before me and that I would be in God's kingdom.

On the flip side, if I knew my time of death was near, I would be concerned for the loved ones left behind. Even though I know that their life will go on without me, I would still be worried and feel sad about the adjustments that they will need to make to a life without me. This would be especially true if my death were sudden. I would hate to think of my loved ones being in pain...the pain I have felt from the loss of a loved one.

Judith Daley is a retired preschool director deeply devoted to her husband of forty-three years, Bill. They have three children and six grandchildren. She still strives to help young children have a positive early childhood learning experience but now instead of a classroom of unrelated children, her passions are focused on her grandchildren. She still hears from her former students and their parents and finds great pleasure in comments sharing positive recollections of their first school experiences.

David Davis—Carry Their Souls: After 9/11

Despite the president calling for a "return to normalcy" and suggesting that the public "go out shopping," I find myself a changed man.

How can one ignore the countless stories of rescue efforts made that day, and in the weeks that followed? Selfless acts of heroism carried out by firefighters, police, and emergency workers (the real heart and soul that this great city was built upon), entering skyscrapers that would soon be leveled. Not to mention the numerous ordinary citizens assisting others to safety, at the risk of their own lives. If that isn't the epitome of a true hero, I don't know what is.

No, Mr. President, with all due respect, from this day forward I've chosen to "carry the souls" of others who didn't make it out that day— on my shoulders, as a firefighter would—giving them the life they so honorably deserve. One that was snuffed out prematurely. A father who will never witness his newborn's first birthday. A mother who won't get the chance to watch her daughter's high school graduation. Individuals with dreams and aspirations. A life I now feel compelled to finish for them, to be filled with exponential vigor, passion, and strength. It's a different world, and I am rising to the occasion. It's the least I can do for the survivors of those families most directly affected.

Dave Davis is a 50-year old preschool teacher for the Head Start Program based at the Children's Museum of the East End in Bridgehampton, NY. His work with special needs children and their families was the inspiration for a recent screenplay titled, Everybody Knew—chosen as the season finale for an award-winning web-series Front Seat Chronicles. His passions include surfcasting, road-trips, and a worldwide search for the ultimate buttered salt bagel.

David Dooley—The Fundamental Divide in Confronting Death

Facing death, it is something we all must do. And no two of us are the same as we do it. But it seems to me that there exists a fundamental divide as we confront death. We either believe that life is irrevocably terminated by death, or that it is not. In some fashion, all the emotions that may accompany our confrontations with death—fear, remorse, despair, abandonment, or feelings of love, hope, friendship, peace— derive from the side of that divide on which we stand at the moment. This is not to say, for me at least, that these sets of emotions are mutually exclusive. I have experienced all of these feelings at funerals and in the days leading up to, and away from, that culminating ritual of passage.

I must also acknowledge that my perspective has been shaped by the lack of opportunity to say goodbye to those to whom I was closest. Especially with my father, there was much that was unfinished and unsaid. I remain uncertain that what I believe is true. What I believe is this: life does not end at death; we shall see one another again. I believe that God created all of us for the joy of life with Him. And that gives me hope—the hope to continue, to overcome despair, and to seek to make this life better, for our efforts are not ultimately meaningless. I suppose that if I did not believe in that, I would not truly believe in anything.

David Dooley became President of the University of Rhode Island in 2009. Prior to joining the University, Dr. Dooley was the provost and vice president for Academic Affairs at Montana State University. He has been active in teaching and research throughout his academic career. Dr. Dooley's wife, Lynn Baker-Dooley, is a Baptist minister. The couple has two adult children, Chris and Samantha, and a dog named Rhody.

David Fogarty—Grounded in the Four Gospels

For me, a sense of accomplishment, or fulfillment, develops over time. I must first choose some goal of value, for example developing a friendship with a person whom I respect or completing an important project or projects in my job, producing technical books. The satisfaction comes when I stay with it, for years if necessary, finding my way around roadblocks and taking advantage of opportunities.

In facing my final accounting at the end of life, which can happen for any of us at any time, I don't consider only my present activities and successes for my sense of worth or satisfaction. Senior citizens, and now, at 72, I am one of them, deserve respect for a lifetime of effort with successes and failures along the way. Our culture often puts too much importance on the latest, best cultural or technological development while ignoring the foundations and those seniors who built them. I must guard against thinking like the culture—what have you done for us recently. Instead, I should think long term—how has my whole life affected all those with whom I have come in contact directly or indirectly: my wife of 43 years, my three children and their children, my five siblings, those I have worked with in book publishing for over 45 years, the students and professionals who buy our books, and my neighbors and the members of my local church parish. Have I treated them the way that I would like to be treated?

For meaning and for values on which to base my life choices I read widely on current questions, but I feel grounded in the four Christian Gospels and the psalms and prophets of Hebrew Scriptures.

David Fogarty is a father and grandfather in his early seventies. When he can find time he enjoys gardening, woods walks, and canoeing. He has been married for forty-three years to Susan Maguire, and they have two sons and one daughter. Their oldest son teaches English in Brazil and he and his Brazilian wife have two young bilingual sons. David and Susan's daughter has worked in book publishing and is now focused on raising her young daughter with another child on the way. Their youngest son is an artist with international artistic admirers. During most weekdays, David is still an editing manager for a publisher of technical books in New York.

Susan Fogarty—Importance of Belonging

In trying to deal with death, a theme I can trace through various situations in my life is a search for community. During the time we have lived in Rutherford, I became involved in the local Interfaith Council—-a group of lay people who belonged to the synagogue and churches in town.

Besides holding monthly meetings, interfaith services and community forums on various topics, the group created a volunteer service which drives people to medical appointments (a service which is still operating after 33 years.) Another "spin-off" which involved hundreds of people from Rutherford and nearby towns was the CROP walk for Church World Service aid and development programs; this was held annually from 1982 through 2011.

Through these activities I have met several close personal friends of different races and religions. I enjoy the meetings as well as the projects, because a sense of belonging is important to me.

Susan Maguire Fogarty, age 70, is the wife of David Fogarty, mother of three and grandmother of three. She enjoys reading, water exercise, baking, and volunteer work. Until June 2012 she had worked for 25 years in a preschool, where she especially enjoyed teaching the children songs.

Hauwa Ibrahim—Do Not Weep For Me—
I Find Meaning in Faith

Faced with the real possibility of death years ago, defending women sentenced to death by stoning in Northern Nigeria, I turned my direction to deep prayer. My prayers—clients, oh Lord, they are powerless and poor—the heart I have supported, ready to pay a price—content to die if doing good should slay me, for I wanted to champion the cause, for if I ceased, then I would not be me. Hugging my children every day as if it's the last day, giving roses and sharing good words and laughter, I found comfort in the verse,"To the righteous soul will be said" "O (thou) soul in complete rest and satisfaction. Enter (thou) My Heaven. Enter (thou) among my devotees (89:27-30).

I find meaning in faith—"...things hoped for, the evidence of things not seen..."Keeping God's commandments—the whole duty of man—fear the LORD, wait on him—to the soul that seeketh the Almighty God and wait, do justly, their strength will be renewed, I rest. Making every effort to add to my faith goodness; knowledge; self-control; perseverance, godliness and love.

So I will say—If I die I don't want anyone to cry for me. I have lived a full life. Weep not for me, but hold fast to the love, the stars will continue to shine and so brightly in my heavenly abode. I may be in the wind in the trees, in the song of birds, or in a glorious rainbow. I am not gone for I will still be around. Let me die the way I want to die, doing what I know is right to do: GOOD. For, from the rising of the sun to its going down, fulfillment in life is to do good.

Hauwa Ibrahim is a Researcher and Visiting Lecturer on Women's Studies and Islamic Law at the Women's Studies in Religion Program at Harvard University's Divinity School. Her latest book is <u>Practicing Shariah Law: Seven Strategies for Achieving Justice in Shariah Courts</u> *published by the American Bar Association in 2013.*

Thomas Keefe–Life as a Path to Experiencing the Divine

Mortality is a gift. It is not 'in the face of death' that I find meaning, but because of it. Mortality gives me context. My life is my opportunity, it is my allotted time.

I know that after my time here on Earth, I will return to God. I know that this life is but a part of my eternal life. This life, however, is also qualitatively different from the next. While union with God is the emphasis in the next life, in this life the emphasis is on our relationship with God. This life is an opportunity to become self-aware, to know others and to know God. This life is a path to experiencing the Divine.

I see myself a part of a continuum; one piece in the greater genealogy of humanity. As I participate in the awesome responsibility to nurture all our children in their own self-awareness and awareness of the Divine, I am also the product of my parents and all those who have influenced me. I believe that the meaning and fulfillment in this life comes from participating in the continuum of humanity and reconciling my temporal self with the unique and eternal expression of God within me.

Tom Keefe has been an educator for fifteen years and currently teaches social studies at the Prout School in Wakefield, RI. He is in the process of writing his dissertation on Stakeholder Understanding of Catholic Educational Mission. Tom is also passionate about peace studies, including awareness of genocide, reconstruction and reconciliation as well as the personal and communal effects of dehumanization. Although he has travelled to more than 24 countries and across the United States, Tom's most rewarding experience has been to know and nurture his children, TJ and Grace Keefe.

Connie Nicolosi—God or No God

The invincible law of life: death, pain. In all of Life's magnificence, is this all there is? Are we merely two-legged primates, part of the evolutionary chain? Are the scientific facts irrefutable? Is there truly no afterlife?

Given my drilled-in Catholic indoctrination, the idea of God is etched in my brain. But still in the face of Science, the thought of nothing more after this haunts me. Have I "wasted" my whole life praying, talking, and thanking a God that doesn't exist? Why, at 70, am I asking myself these questions, when I should be on my knees praying for a fast and easy death?

Here's the thing: When it comes to the meaning of life and fulfillment, if God exists, no sweat: Whether Christian, Jew, Muslim, Buddhist, Mormon or whatever, just abide by whatever your Good Book says. Have faith; bear your burdens and the voids of loss with acceptance; love, give of yourself to family, friends, and all in need; save the planet; be kind to animals, enjoy the pleasures of art, music, literature, the wonders of the world your God has created. Ecstasy will be your reward.

Aah...but what if there is no god? Where are meaning and fulfillment? Life is an excellent thing; it is brutal; it isn't fair, but warts and all, it's still a good thing. To paraphrase Dante, the mean of life is to hand down a legacy so that generations can improve upon it with a thirst for knowledge, with a passion—not for money or things—but to show others another road.

As for me, I'm playing it safe and following both paths. If there is a God, He'll save a place at His table for me. If not, then perhaps others will remember me with a smile...and take that other road.

A veteran IBMer, now marketing communications consultant and world traveler, Concetta Nicolosi happily enjoys life near the Rhode Island shoreline. A lifelong learner, she studies Italian history and literature at Providence College, as well as enjoys the Italian arts, culture, and people during her annual trips to Italy. Regarding life in our world today, she cites Teilhard de Chardin, "Someday, after we have mastered the winds, the waves, the tides and gravity, we shall harness for God the energies of love. Then, for the second time in the history of the world, man will have discovered fire."

Michael V. Pearce–Learning to Regret

As life is temporary, we face death from conception. If people live a life of illusion and do not embrace the reality of their own morality until they are actually at the doorstep of death, then the likelihood of finding fulfillment is less probable. However, individuals who embrace their mortality and can identify both their achievements and failures throughout their existence are far more likely to find both peace and fulfillment.

Human beings are imperfect creatures who often seek to find fulfillment in very narrow forms of self-gratification. Therefore, I believe that merely placing one's achievements in a metaphorical trophy box is both dangerous and daft. A person's worth cannot be measured solely by occupational or educational achievements, works of charity, or even devotion to a deity. A person's worth is also measured by failures and regrets, and whether or not he or she has embraced them fully.

Life is about constant reflection, and if we possess the humility to identify our short fallings and remedy them, we have turned failure into a success of sorts. St. Augustine taught that out of evil can come good. So, I would suggest that in the face of death we must not only look at our acts of "pure good", but how we dealt with (or continue to deal with) those instances when we chose evil.

Ultimately, our lives are not measured merely by our accomplishments, but also by those things we regret, as our misdeeds will often outweigh the good. If we leave our misdeeds in the past and do not take the time to reconcile them (or even regret them, for that matter), then our failures become exponential with each day. However, we can transform our regrets into accomplishments with the proper degree of humility. A human being who does not possess the humility to regret his or her misdeeds has lived a life of illusion and will find neither peace nor fulfillment.

Michael V. Pearce is currently a rating specialist with the U.S. Department of Veterans Affairs. He served honorably in the U.S. Marine Corps (1988-92), and earned a B.A. in Political Science from the University of Rhode Island (1996) and an M.Ed. in Educational Administration from Tarleton State University (2006). He is a devout Catholic and is active in Republican politics. He currently lives in central Texas with his wife and 6 children.

Jean Revil—Death Is Merely a Change of Address

Knowing that life on this earth is not forever, adds a sense of urgency to finding meaning and fulfillment. There is not a lot of time to waste! Ultimately, our deepest meaning and greatest fulfillment will always be connected to our experiences of self-giving love. This is what Jesus taught as He encouraged his followers to deny themselves, to die to themselves. This is such a counter-cultural instruction, then and now.

As a Catholic Christian, I find the meaning of my life in my relationship with Jesus Christ. It is in a relationship where the deepest meaning and sense of fulfillment is found. We are social by design, created by God who is Himself pure relationship—Father, Son and Spirit. Life is so precious because we share it with those we love. Love requires us to make choices based on the good of the ones we love, not our own selfish desires. Each act of love brings us closer to the source of love—God. As one who believes in eternal life, death is merely a change of address. Relationships do not end with death, love does not end with death, only the expression changes.

Jean Revil is a Benedictine Oblate and this is her 34th year of teaching at Bishop Stang High School in Fall River, Massachusetts where she has served as Director of Campus Ministry and as the Theology Department Chairperson. She teaches Theology III which explores the sacramental prayer life of the Catholic Church and personal morality. She also teaches Thanatology, examining the physical, emotional, social and spiritual aspects of death and dying.

Arthur Stein—Soul's Journey Homeward

As the Buddha among others reminds us, it is in the nature of all sentient beings to die. Yet this inevitable event in no way diminishes the significance of each person's life, or its countless effects on posterity for many generations to come.

The transitional passage called death can be envisioned as a most meaningful time in our lives. When my days are coming to an end, I hope to be fully conscious, welcoming this natural event with equanimity and without fear, and with a prayer of thanksgiving in my heart for the gift of life here on Mother Earth. I'll also be grateful for a loving family, friendships and for moments such as this—sitting here on my back porch on a crisp, autumnal morning pondering a profound question that has been posed.

Here very briefly is a composite view, drawn from a number of the world's mystical/spiritual traditions, of what may be the next stage(s) or phase(s) of the soul's journey homeward: In the transition that follows physical death, the epicenter of human consciousness (most commonly referred to cross-culturally as the soul) rises phoenix-like from the lifeless physical body. Creatively envisage the soul becoming "enrolled" in a new "school" appropriate for its further development. And thereafter, that this "tutelage" process could continue anew in a series of "venues." These learning experiences could involve a return(s) to earth in various reincarnations. Yet eventually the soul experiencing pangs of separation, would yearn to reach beyond the realms of time and space, to directly experience "celestial Light and Love" at their source.

In the Jewish tradition there is a saying which in effect declares: If we do our best to live our lives with integrity in this world, *h'olam ha zah*, then the world to come, *h'olam ha boh*, will take care of itself. This recognition has become increasingly meaningful to me as the years pass by.

Returning to the here and now, the values which each of us uphold in daily life are more vital than we often realize—for personal fulfillment and for the overall well-being of humankind and all life-forms within our shared planetary home. With this in mind, let me offer in grateful remembrance a few verses on *ahimsa*-nonviolence that came to me, inspired by the insights of a beloved pioneer of human unity, Sant Kirpal Singh (1894-1974). Teaching by personal example, he gave fresh meaning to the simple words "little, little things."

AHIMSA

Those little, little things
Go a long, long way
Unkind thoughts and hurtful words
Add to the turmoil in the world
All the precepts high and lofty
Pale outside the light of Love
Children mirror what they see
And tune out truths that ring untrue
Compassion for each humble life form
Hear the needy's plaintive call
Love not measured out in meters
Given freely, comes back home
Give balm to lacerated hearts
And cloak the storm- drenched soul
That has not felt healing warmth
Kindled by thy loving Word
This Word is not enshrined in stone
Nor subject to the tides of time
But wherever hearts are yearning
Dwells within the human shrine
Yes, those little, little things,
Do go a long, long way
Each kind word and caring deed
Brings joy and peace to humankind

This year, 2014, marks a half-century of teaching for Arthur Stein at the University of Rhode Island. He says he has been fortunate to have had many fine colleagues and, as a lifetime learner, has come to truly know that "from my students I've been taught." Art's "redirection" (not retirement) involves helping out the Center for Nonviolence and Peace Studies at the University of Rhode Island, locally and globally—while learning to walk more lightly and appreciatively on the earth.

Bishop Thomas Tobin—Without Immortality, the Specter of Death Would Be Terrifying

From a Christian perspective, no one should be intimated by the thought of death. I often find consolation in the Book of Wisdom, often used at Catholic funerals: "The souls of the just are in the hand of God, and no torment shall touch them. They seemed, in the view of the foolish to be dead, but they are in peace." This Old Testament insight is affirmed by Jesus in the New Testament: "I am the resurrection and the life; whoever believes in me, even if he dies, will live."

My faith makes the difference—in the way I live and the way I will die. If I didn't believe in the immortality of the human soul, my journey here on earth would be rather pointless, and the specter of death would be terrifying. But I believe in eternal life. Therefore I strive to live my life in harmony with the inspiration of my faith. I believe that good deeds will be rewarded and that sin will be punished. And I believe that when I fall short, God forgives me. In the end, I will throw myself on the mercy of the divine court, knowing that the Heavenly Judge is rich in wisdom, understanding and forgiveness.

Finally, I see death as a welcome respite from the trials and tribulations of life. My epitaph could very well be: "I've worked hard and done my best. Now it's time to get some rest."

The Most Reverend Thomas J. Tobin was named Bishop of the Diocese of Providence, Rhode Island in 2005. Prior to his Providence appointment, he was an Auxiliary Bishop of Pittsburgh, Pennsylvania (1992-1995) and was later consecrated as Bishop of Youngstown, Ohio (1995-2005.) In addition to his priestly duties in Pittsburgh, he was born there—all of which probably accounts for his continued and avid support of the Pittsburgh Steelers though he now lives and ministers deep in New England Patriots country.

Mark Wimbush–Die Before Dying

Our lifespan is limited. You know when it began; you don't know when it will end—but you're aware there will be a day beyond which you have no conscious, no physical presence in the world. Perhaps we're the only creatures who have that knowledge. It urges me to find out why I'm here and what I need to accomplish during this life. A Sufi teaching says, "Die before dying": what will be apparent when I die, I should strive to learn now while I have time to use that knowledge. I must love God and my neighbour. In dying, I hope to know my presence in the world has, at the very least, brought my fellow humans more happiness than harm. For each of us, death should be an act not of defeasance but of fulfillment, a time to step gladly and confidently across the threshold into Christ's presence and life eternal.

Having meandered from Kenya to the USA—with waypoints in the UK and Japan—Mark Wimbush settled, with his wife Reiko, in Rhode Island 36 years ago. Although technically retired, he's still enjoying research in physical oceanography and is not yet ready to give it up. Nevertheless, he's trying to cultivate his right cerebral hemisphere by attending Reiko's art history classes.

CHAPTER 5

When A Loved One Dies

Death ends a life, not a relationship.
—Robert Benchley

John Bayerl—A Final Dressing

This is something I remember vividly and lovingly about the night Gwen died. Gwen and I had discussed having me bathe and dress her in clean clothes after her death. As events transpired, I was able to honor her in that way. It is my most loving memory of that whole evening.

I filled a basin with warm water, being careful that it was neither too cold nor too hot. (I would treat her no differently in death than I had in life.) I removed her clothing, soaped a washcloth and gave her a final bath. Then I sprayed on a little of her favorite perfume, patted on some of her favorite "Youth Dew" dusting powder, dressed her in some favorite clothing. I was able to prepare her for her last journey. It was the loving thing to do. My memories of this are so tender, personal and poignant that to attempt to describe them in more detail would make them meaningless. The poem below tries to capture a little bit of what it felt like:

FIRST AND LAST MOMENTS

I hold her lifeless body
In my warm embrace,
a soft sigh of false hope escapes her lips
as I gently raise and bathe her.

I hold in my arms
the same loving body
I beheld with wonder
on our first night together.

She was soft and giving then,
when our lives as one began,
sharing our love,
completing each other.

Her beautiful blue eyes, now closed,
filled with tears of joy
on that first night
as she gave me all her warmth.
Now, it is my eyes that fill with tears.

John A. Bayerl was born and raised on a farm near Menominee in Michigan's Upper Peninsula. He completed a B. A. degree in Education at Northern Michigan University and M. A. and Ph.D. Degrees in School Guidance and Counseling at the University of Michigan. In June of 1963 John married Gwendolyn Bartczak, and they enjoyed a marriage of 47 years, raising four children. In November of 2010 John lost his dear wife to cancer. By accepting and dealing with his pain and grief following the death of his wife, John made room in his heart for a new love, and in June of 2012 he met Jann, whom he married in October of 2013.

William F. Daley, Jr.–Celebrating the Love of Those Lost

I have always been "ok" with the idea of death. For no particular reason, it has always been something that I have accepted in life, even from a very early age. I have always known that I will die, that my family and friends will die, and that it has always been, and always will be a part of life. I can't really say why I have been so understanding about the inevitability of death and dying, but perhaps it was because when I was younger, I was an altar boy at my local Catholic parish and participated in weekly funerals. Perhaps this is why I have not been deeply affected by death and loss emotionally, I have never really had to deal with the death of anybody close to me until very recently, in the later years of my life. In the last 10 years I have lost three people very close to me, all being very important people in my life, and people that had a profound influence on me as a person. The deaths of these three people were very different, both in how and when they died, and how I was able to say goodbye, or in one case was unable to do so. The first two were my grandmothers. Obviously both extremely close family members, and both huge influences on my life. Although it was very difficult to lose both of them, I again knew that their deaths, like everyone else's, were inevitable.

Both of my grandmothers died at a considerable old-age, and had lived very exciting and fulfilled lives. They did not suffer in the days leading up to their death, and in many ways they themselves knew it was "their time to go." That said, what I found to be the most rewarding opportunity in the days leading up to the moment they died, was the fact that I was able to sit by their bedside and reflect on the wonderful joys they brought to me in my life. I essentially was allowed to say thank you to them with a goodbye. Although I hated to see them go, and even though I miss them, it was a way to have peace with their passing by being able to have closure and to be able to say, "I love you."

Unfortunately, the other person I lost recently was one of my very best friends, and I did not have the opportunity to say goodbye. He died suddenly, at age 39, for no reason that can be explained except that his heart malfunctioned. He did not drink or smoke, was in great shape, and was a wonderful husband and father of two young boys. That is when death can sneak up and baffle, when it isn't something natural or accepted. I can say that initially after his death that was the case—unacceptable. However, as time went on, I did realize that no matter what, we will all leave and there really isn't anything anyone can do about it. We cannot choose when, where, or how. I have accepted that he is gone, and now all I can do is celebrate his memory by remembering his stories, his funny moments, and his pictures. That is what I believe to be the meaning of death itself—celebrating the love of those lost. That is what keeps life moving on.

William Daley, Jr. was born in Boston, and remains a passionate advocate of his birth city and the great history within the surrounding New England area. An avid sports fan, he is a huge supporter of the Boston Bruins. For the past 13 years he has had a successful career as a writer and producer in the television and film production industry. His proudest accomplishment is being an uncle to six amazing nieces and nephews.

James Findlay–Lessons from Losing A Son

S truggling with the problem of death first thrust itself upon me in concrete ways twenty-eight years ago during the long struggle to save, then to lose, our son Peter to leukemia. That process took three + years and deeply affected the entire Findlay family. Now that I am 81 and facing my own death in the near future, I reflect on that earlier experience and realize that it suggested powerful dimensions to human experience that helped us through then, and still will, I believe, enable me to retain a sense of hope and meaning in my life until I leave permanently this "vale of tears."

First, the earlier experience underscored the critical fact of friendships and close personal relationships that made it possible to go about our daily lives and to live constructively. We were surrounded with three circles of support and love, one in Indiana where I first taught and where my wife and I still maintain our deepest friendships, the second among my colleagues at the University of Rhode Island, the third in our local church, Kingston Congregational (U.C.C.). Those circles of human connections still undergird our lives. They will remain so, I am certain, until I die. Closely related to these friends, the ultimate friend in my life, is my wife. I am free to confess to her my deepest fears and longings; we can disagree, but arguments carry no lasting effects and often enable us both to gain new insights and acceptances about ourselves and other people. Such daily support and love from another is central to my ability to continue to find "meaning and fulfillment" in my waning years.

Second, from the Peter experience there emerged new thrusts of energy and personal commitment that created in my private and professional life new dimensions and reinforced other long-held attitudes and beliefs that reached back into my childhood. Both my wife and I purposely maintained our jobs throughout the crisis, knowing that essential daily routines needed to be maintained. The same is true now, although the routine has changed quite a bit. At the close of the struggle with Peter I altered my research interests and, knowing that Peter approved, began a new project. That project ended in a book that is still in print. Peter wrote a will just before he died which has resulted in an annual jazz concert for the student body at the local high school, and an annual college scholarship, to be awarded to a student exhibiting unusual interest in "social justice issues." These positive outcomes of death shape both my wife and me even today, providing us with hope and a belief in constructive action that will influence us until WE die.

Finally, the experience with Peter reinforced my long-held religious beliefs as the ground of my being, as a source of comfort and hope as life on this earth comes to an end. My belief system surely is less "simple Christian" than it once was, but I still hold that God is present in the world, that love for the world and all of us therein reflects His/Her essence, that God is steadfast (a frequently used term in the Book of Psalms) in His/Her support of us. Beliefs such as these, plus my continuing participation in the deeply meaningful worship and life of my local congregation, provide me some of the means to possibly "die well" when that moment comes.

Jim Findlay is a persistent gardener, enjoys grocery shopping and cooking, summer "intergenerational" trips with his grandchildren, volunteer work in South Providence, daily walks on the beach, Starbucks iced coffee, reading, listening to jazz and classical music. Variety keeps life interesting. Church life, his wife, and good friends are the guideposts to a long life.

Joanne Mazzotta—Grief and Love, A Son's Suicide

I am the mother of four adult children; three of whom walk and one who flies.

My way of finding meaning and fulfillment in life after a mother's worst fear was realized, was to give my grief a voice and disarm it.

In the quiet, painfully lonely days and nights after the death of my son, I wrote to an invisible entity that seemed intent on winning a battle I was not prepared to fight. I found myself needing to live on for my family and needing to understand what grief could do to me if I let it. I learned after many failures that to suffer for what you cannot change is fate. To suffer for what you can change is choice. When I surrendered completely to shock, guilt, anger, depression, I disarmed my grief. I was then able to thank my son for coming into my life, and continue to love him while clearing the path to love itself for my family and eight grandchildren and finding my path back to harmony in my own life.

Because Danny committed suicide, there may be an engraved stain on my life, but I am no longer enraged by it. Grief has value, and that value will abide. It cannot deprive us of love. It can only pay reverence to love and remind us to pay respect to all life.

Joanne Mazzotta is the mother of four adult children, the grandmother of eight, and wife of a wonderful man. She is the former owner of five restaurants, an oil paint artist, and author of a book called WHY WHISPER? Her book is a collection of journals written after the suicide of her 32 year old son. She devotes much of her time speaking to those who need a place to turn after losing a loved one to suicide. She has spoken on numerous talk radio programs across the country and Canada, three WPRI News Street Stories, and to University of Rhode Island adult education classes—endorsing a right to be heard to suicide grief while erasing the stigma and offering support.

Monica May Glushanok–Requiem for Henry Saia

My husband, Peter Glushanok, composed a requiem for his dear friend Henry Saia after Henry took his own life. Henry opened the door to immortality unbidden and walked away from his life, loves and friendships.

Peter took Henry's last despairing call and, because he had not been able to go to him in time to perhaps save him, and so that Henry would not have to journey all alone on that road from which no one has ever returned, Peter composed a Requiem and when Henry heard it, he wanted to return for a moment in time, but, his journey had already begun and he was not able to take even one step back so that Henry could embrace his true friend once more.

But when mortality meets immortality on that journey to Hades and where Henry would meet other kindred souls, he entered with dignity because Peter's Requiem was a loving companion on the awesome journey from which no one has ever returned. Requiem for Henry Saia won 1st prize at the Dartmouth College Second International Arts Council.

I married Peter sometime after Henry's sad departure from this world. One evening, when we were in Peter's huge studio in one of those cavernous apartments on Riverside Drive, Peter said "let me play something that I composed as a requiem for Henry Saia". This was the time of the beginning of electronic New Age Music, and so Peter wanted to share with me his feelings of loss because Henry had been part of this venture. The music was so beautiful, so haunting, so yearning. And then, I wrote "my" obituary for Henry Saia—a man I never met except in the knowledge that he was loved.

Monica May Glushanok was born in Glasgow Scotland in 1923 to peripatetic Irish parents. She spent her early years touring the industrial cities of Northern England and the Bogs of Co. Tipperary, the family arriving in London just in time for WWII and the adventures of the Blitz. She was deliriously happy to be married to the composer, painter, photographer and filmmaker Peter Glushanok who composed the Requiem for his friend Henry Saia. She retired to Wakefield, RI in 2004 where she reads, writes and philosophizes regularly.

Ann McIntyre–Death of a Child

No! No! No! It can't be It mustn't be.
O My God. Wailing. Retching. Tears.

It can't be true.
If only. Regrets. Restless nights,
Worse days. I can't do this.
Where are You My God?

Then the Crescent moon, First star at night.
A deep sigh. I will be okay. Maybe.
My God You are here. More tears.

Then memories, Too many memories.
Your face, Your smile, Your laughter.
Only memories left. Days pass. Nights are longer.
Then a little peace. A daisy, A gentle breeze.
A smile. A hug. A few tears, Always tears.

Time passes slowly. The tears are fewer.
The grief melts into sadness. My God has heard me.
The daisies have done their magic. The gentle breeze caresses me.
The hugs have brought some healing. Shrunk just a bit the hole
    in my heart.

My family has held me till I can breathe on my own.
My friends have taken my hands lovingly.
I live with my memories but not all painful ones.
I can breath easier, more naturally.
The tears are more often in my heart now

But I am changed.
You will always be with me. Frozen in time.
I am loving and believing again.
I watch the children play.

I can spend time with My God. I will live.
But you will always be with me.
And There will always be tears.
There will always be tears.

Ann McIntyre was born in Chicago. Her parents, Mary and James Houlihan, gave her life and so much more. A love of all people came from her father and the desire to seek, to question, and to do, came from her mother. She and her husband, Jack, have five children. Katie, her third, died three months into life from multiple birth defects. "She was a beautiful baby, blue eyes and strawberry blond hair. We miss her still. From her life and death, I have learned that babies, all babies, are gifts from God and need to be loved, honored, cared for and tickled."

William Morgan—The Purpose of Life Is Not Only to Live for Oneself

After losing my grandfather and aunt in a matter of only nine months I was forced to face a question that so many have faced before. How do we find meaning in life when our time is so uncertain? When it can end so much sooner than expected? The saying "to live each day like it's your last" simply seems insufficient. While it is true that the meaning of life cannot be found in the time we are given, but rather is defined by what we do with the time that is given to us, the meaning of life is far more complex than the saying would have us believe. The meaning of life can be found in our passions and in our fears, in our laughs and in our tears, in our words and in our deeds. The purpose of life is not only to live for oneself, but to live for the pursuit of something larger than oneself—to fight injustice, defend the weak, or love a child. At the end of our days, whenever it may come, a successful life is not measured by the balance in our bank account or the size of our home. Instead, success is measured by the number of people whose lives we have touched, the number of people who say that their lives have changed for the good because of us.

William Morgan is a graduate of UMass-Boston where he received a degree in English with a concentration in Creative Writing. He was instructed there in several writing courses by poets Martha Collins and Lloyd Schwartz. He served as assistant editor of the Dorchester Community News. Bill's most notable previous publication is the poem "Family Christmas" in Amador Publishers' anthology 'Christmas Blues: Behind the Holiday Mask.' He is a resident of Arlington, MA.

Susie Hemingway Mourisi—The Way to Affirmation

I was married to my only love for almost thirty years and after a bravely fought battle to survive, Hamada lost his fight for life in November 2010. Caregivers are exhausted after much time and many years in some cases. We do for others what we might never dream of doing for ourselves and the struggle is hard, as this good man had the strongest will to live! We bravely go beyond barriers unknown to us. We fight battles, challenge medical authorities to negotiate the best care possible. Hamada fought every step of the way to continue to stay with us, accepting every treatment available, as many do. After his death I recalled the wise words of this clever man, these words spoken during his illness and a lot towards the end, requesting that I continue to live my life well and with joy. Difficult yes! But affirming life in the face of death is just that, the most difficult and painful road in the highway of life. How easy it would be to succumb and hide away with my grief as I know many choose to do. I so wanted that at times, feeling that I had nothing more to live for, but the dawn rises every day when all else is lost and for me it would have been a dishonor to this amazing man who fought through every treatment to survive. Affirmation! Yes a serious and solemn declaration of affection for the essence of this good man.

I decided as my body returned to life once more, that I would honor my husband's memory and go forth with joy and a smile on my face and live the life he so wanted to do.

Embracing the years I have left in the best way I can, will be my affirmation. Watching and absorbing all that he can no longer see or do. Knowing and learning more about this world we live in and accepting my life now with the joy he taught me when we were together. No it will never be the same, but it will be the best I can do without him. It will be mastered in his honor.

Before affirmation, come the shock, the numbness, denial, depression, fear and then acceptance. Only when you accept and only then, can you affirm life in the aftermath of death. Hamada loved to have fun and so shall I. The smile on my face will be the affirmation of my life lived with him; all we achieved together, all he taught me about living and what a waste if I do not make the most of these remaining years in the best way I can. Affirmation of a life lived well in his loving memory.

Susie Hemingway Moursi has always written poetry, but began publishing on-line when her husband Hamada Moursi was diagnosed with Multiple Myeloma and given just six months to live. Her two blogs http://www. susiehemingway.blogspot.com/ and http://www.susiehemingway.com/ talk about their life and love. Susie is a published poet. She has also written the book "A Power Within". She is the mother of two adult sons and one grandson. She lives in the Lincolnshire Wolds, UK. Hamada passed away in 2010 after a five year battle with Multiple Myeloma.

Wayne Olson—Me and Job

Job was a rich man; I am not. Job was a perfect man in God's sight; I am not. Job "eschewed evil"' I wish I could say that about me, but I cannot. One thing I do aspire to with respect to Job, and may be a point of honest comparison, is his claim, "Though he slay me, yet will I trust." Job was, of course as his story goes, quite slain. In a pact with the Devil, God permitted Satan to do whatever he wished to Job to test his faith, so Job lost family, house, property, wealth, and health. But Job professed his utmost trust in God, even in the midst of those dire circumstances. Not even the Devil could persuade him to denounce God. The story has lived all these centuries in Scripture and in our culture. We have honored him with the expression common among believers and nonbelievers alike, "the patience of Job."

Job was unaware that he was the victim of this seemingly cruel pact, and I wonder if his faith would have been so secure had he known that it was God's fault that he suffered so. He did not ask God, as Jesus did, "Why have you forsaken me?" It never occurred to him that God might be behind his sudden and dreadful misfortunes. The ultimate moral of the Job story is that God can outsmart the Devil, that Good {God} triumphs over Bad, even in the midst of human suffering. That God permitted Job to suffer so remains a huge theological issue, but it is clear God did not cause the suffering. That is comforting.

So now in my eightieth year, I find myself suffering, not nearly to the extent to which Job suffered, but faced nevertheless with health issues that in all likelihood will lead to my death. I have this wonderful advantage over Job—I still have family, home, doctors, medicines, friends, and love, especially from my wife who makes every day easier than it might otherwise be. All of these blessings compensate beyond compare to the pain and suffering my body inflicts upon me. I feel ashamed when I allow myself to concentrate on the negatives rather than on the positives. As I wrote above, unlike Job you see, I am not a perfect man.

Cancer is a murderer, and the medical world wages war upon it daily. It is better to be fighting it now than it would have been several decades ago. There are cancer survivors everywhere among us. I see them on every visit I make to the cancer treatment center. I see them in the shops and on streets of the towns we visit. I see them in the pews of my church. Job did not have such luxury. He fought it alone.

Unlike Job I have had many bouts with doubt about God. I still do. It took me a long time to know the God I know now. I do not think God evolved in Job's mind; the story does not suggest that. It suggests rather that Job's faith was secure from the beginning. Maybe that kept him from the temptation to concentrate on the negatives of woe as I am wont to do at times. For in all candor, if there be one thing I am jealous of with respect to Fundamentalist Christians it is their sense of assurance, their confidence in their faith. I have never had that, but I am coming to it now, although in a quite different context and style from theirs, and certainly from Job's. I know whom I have believed, and I know whom I now believe. And while they are One and the Same, they are vastly different from the way they started.

God is a metaphor now, never was before. God stands for all that is good and holy and decent and redemptive. God is beauty in art, music, literature, nature, and wherever there is an ennobling of the culture or the environment. God is love, as the Bible correctly claims, and that love is what I find in wife, children, and friendships. God is memory, seen as I look around the house that has become our home, filled with reminders of moments too sacred to forget. God has allowed my life to be filled with adventures, acquaintances, and activities that speak of Providential guidance, Divine interventions unacknowledged at the time. Nothing in all creation separates God from all this, not even cancer. And God is forgiveness, best illustrated in the life, death and resurrection of Jesus, who unlike Job, was perfect and loved even His enemies.

So, though God slay me with cancer, yet will I trust. I can say this now as Job said it in time past. I asked the doctor what caused it, knowing he did not know, but I was both surprised and pleased with his answer: "Bad luck." There is no judgment there, no accusation of bad behavior or careless living. Another doctor himself cried when he told Rosemary and our daughter about my condition. There is humanity in the world and it is filled with Divinity, even as some humanity may be filled with the Devil trying to overcome the goodness that is God. Jesus advised that there will be wars and rumors of wars. He may just as well have said there will be cancers and there will be rumors of cancers. In the midst of this mixed up world, as for me and my house, we will serve the Lord, by loving, by caring, by remembering and by believing. If only Job had had his wife at his side, his suffering would have been alleviated a thousand times. Thank you, God, for these gifts of love and beauty that give me hope, faith and comfort in this time.

Dr. Olson was a retired minister in the United Church of Christ as well as a retired Instructor of Speech at Butler University and Indiana-Purdue University at Indianapolis. He was a noted scholar of the New England Transcendentalists including Emerson, Thoreau and Margaret Fuller. He founded the Indiana AIDS Pastoral Care Network. He graduated from Hope College and Western Theological Seminary and received an Ed.D. from Teachers College at Columbia University.

Marisa Quinn—It's Not What You Take, But What You Leave Behind

I think about death often. I plan for it, sometimes obsessively through elaborate details in my will down to the music for any memorial service that may occur post-me. Perhaps my preoccupation is the result of my Irish Catholic upbringing, which included attending many wakes and funerals from a very young age. Being in the presence of a dead body was not that unusual, that is, until it was someone close. I stared at my Nana in her casket when I was 10, touched her ice-cold arthritic hand and wondered if she just may "wake." It was when my mother died when I was 14 that death assumed real and profound meaning, and is no doubt the core of my constant awareness of life's taunting fragility. She warned us, rife with cancer, that she would die, and urged celebration and appreciation over sadness and strife. When a cold February morning rang in with a call from the hospital reporting she had died, it was not real. The memories of those days are a blur, but rather than feeling like I had lost my ballast I learned that my mother had given me everything I needed.

Nearly 35 years later, I am more aware than ever that it is not the duration of a life that matters, but the impact on others. I am the woman I am because of the 14 short years I had with my Mom. I am the wife, mother, friend, sister, aunt and hard worker because of the experience I had with a mother who loved her family and raised us with great care and attention. So, yes, I am prone to obsess about death....the idea of passing too soon and missing all that lies ahead is unbearable. I want to continue to experience the joy—and pain—of raising a child, to see my son navigate college, travel, marry. I want to indulge my future grandchildren in a way my mother never could. I want more trips picking out Christmas trees, more bike rides, more steamy beach days and outdoor showers, more morning coffee. I will never get all I want, that I know. But I also know it's not what you take that is enduring, it's what you leave behind.

Marisa Quinn is VP of Public Affairs and University Relations at Brown University. She has devoted most of her 49 years to loving Rhode Island, venturing off to live in the Philippines, Hawaii, Washington, DC and the NY/NJ area at various points, confirming that—for her—the grass is greener at home. She grew up the youngest of six, learning the essential skills of observation and negotiation that prepared her for a career in politics, policy and higher education administration. She continues to appreciate all the treasures that the Ocean State offers, working at Brown University, spending time enjoying the beauty of her Jamestown home, and being with friends and family.

Evelyn Wight—Keep Going

When my older sister was murdered, I almost died from the pain. I had lost my mother and a girlfriend to suicide, and a boyfriend to a wine-induced car wreck. I wanted out then, but I promised my remaining sister I wouldn't end it.

I didn't die. I raged. I wandered streets in rootless desolation. I passed out in a drunken stupor. I went to work. I was crazy with grief at inopportune moments. I craved friends, and then refused them. I sobbed for years.

I kept on going. Every day. And I tried things. I tried hating. I tried loving plants instead of people. I tried not needing anything or anyone. I tried losing myself in work. I stole a cat who wasn't mine. She came when I called and I clung to her fiercely.

Eventually, I found little things that pleased me: The sound of laughter. New growth on a branch. The purring silky kitty fur under my hands. The angle of light hitting a building at dusk, making me wonder if the architect intended that.

Sometimes I still sob for hours, or days. But for me, life has been made worth living by continuing to find things to love. I press my animal body toward warmth. I forgive myself for surviving. I laugh out loud at silliness. I marvel at butterflies and concrete.

If you're reading this, you didn't die either. And if you're anything like me, you'll feel better, eventually, if you keep going.

Evelyn Wight grew up in six countries (Brazil, Bangladesh, Afghanistan, U.S., Korea, India) with two sisters, an alcoholic father, a schizophrenic mother, and a cruel stepmother. She likes adventure—from backpacking the world in her 20s to moving jobless to Hawaii in her 40s. She once described herself as a pixie with a broken heart, but nowadays she laughs a lot and revels in silliness. She stays focused on moments, forgets insults, and tries to forgive, herself included. She still has bad days and feels scared of her next big loss—it's inevitable after all—but she just keeps going.

Genie Wild—I Won't Get Over It

Fredrika, my daughter, died when she was 16.

During the 13 years from her diagnosis of leukemia until her death, I worked to help her get through. I was honest with her, explanations growing more technical as she grew up. I was with her, comforting her during painful procedures: chemotherapy, bone marrows and spinal taps.

She grew up with her disease and took it in stride. Her plan was "to live until she died" which she did. She went to school hurting and bald. She was top of her class and participated in many activities: drama, violin lessons, editing the school newspaper. She embraced being alive.

She didn't want to die, but she faced the possibility with equanimity. My task was to keep up with her, allowing all that was possible.

I found it hard to help her through what I didn't want her to have to face. I found it hard to find a balance between caring and overprotectiveness. She worked with me, even asking permission to die once when it appeared that death was imminent. "That's what kids do," she said.

Our time together was full.

Since her death I have lived with the loss of her. I won't "get over it" as people think I should; I have adapted. I miss seeing who she would have become, holding her, talking to her.

Genie Wild continues with her counseling practice, valuing being with people through their life crises and joys. She is a volunteer community member of the State of Rhode Island Department of Health Board of Medical Licensure and Discipline. She enjoys her garden and appreciates sharing chores with her son, Ed. She loves going to traditional jazz concerts because of the energy and fun. Connections with friends round out her time. Weekly lunches, trips to the theatre, watercolor classes and even time at the gym continue to enhance her life.

CHAPTER 6

Death And Interconnectedness

"I have loved the stars too fondly to be fearful of the night."
—Galileo

Robert Carothers—The Life Force

The question of finding meaning and fulfillment in the face of death is at the heart of the human experience, of our defining mortality. When I was young, I thought of death as an insult, and everyday picked up Sisyphus' rock as an act that defied death, a deep refusal to yield. Melville's Ahab was my model. As I grew older and learned something of the wisdom of the East, I came to understand better our passage through death and have tried to live my life with calm and good humor in preparation. This is the lesson of Ishmael, who survives the maelstrom floating on a coffin in a deep blue sea. The sea, which can drown us, still holds us up if we do not panic, if we learn to breathe, if we come to understand that we swim with young, leaping dolphins and old sea turtles slowly moving from the shore to the depths and back again. We are not separate from them, nor from the force that created them. I see it from the corner of my eye as it scampers along our stone wall, and hear it in the coyote's call in the dark night. I feel it as the bass school together in the cove. That force flows through us all, and it does not die.

Robert Carothers is a poet who served for eighteen years as the president of the University of Rhode Island. Free from the stresses of that role, he now lives in Saunderstown, Rhode Island, where he writes, gardens and fishes. He has served as mentor for scores of rising deans, provosts and presidents through the Fellows program of the American Council on Education and continues that work. Most importantly, he is the grandfather of eleven brilliant and charming children.

Francis X. Clooney, SJ—Deadlines

Even as a child, I had a sense that the years were quickly passing. I have always been aware of the passing of time and a sense—sometimes vague, sometimes acute—that time is running out. Yet that sense of the transitory was not necessarily gloomy. Rather, it also opened a way for me to appreciate life right now. Meaning and fulfillment have for me always been connected to the gift of the moment: it is enough, and it matters because such moments, and our whole lives, come to an end.

As a scholar too, I find deadlines difficult, since we never have enough time, but extremely helpful too, since they also force me to do the best I can under the circumstances before time runs out. We learn what we can say in our writing—or say imperfectly, or leave as is—unfinished but now published, simply because there is no time left. Such is the article or the book, and such my life, as scholar and person.

Thus far, I have been thinking of me, and to some extent of people close to me, whose lives too are preciously short. But I am also aware of the many shadows of death and ending in our wider world, where the many people live on the edge of death, in places of violence and poverty, confronting death on an immediate and brutal level. Such tragedies are not to be philosophized away. Against this larger background, my small life, content and safe even if finite, evokes a vocation in the face of death, to be and act as one mindful of those who suffer and die even as I write.

I have always been acutely aware of death's sacred meanings. In studying the Hindu traditions for decades, I have been taught that living is dying; nothing lasts, every beginning predicts an ending, and death opens into birth. It is possible to be tranquil in the presence of my sickness, my ageing, and my death, because such is reality. And all in all, I have lived by the mystery basic to my Christian faith, the death of Christ: unless you lose your life, you shall not save it; unless the grain of wheat fall to the ground, it shall not bear fruit. With Christ I die, with him I rise. Such truths matter at the end, but they are writ small too, in all the events and deadlines of everyday life.

Francis X. Clooney, S.J., joined the Harvard Divinity School faculty in 2005. He is Parkman Professor of Divinity and Professor of Comparative Theology and, since 2010, Director of the Center for the Study of World Religions. After earning his doctorate in South Asian languages and civilizations (University of Chicago, 1984), he taught at Boston College for 21 years before moving to Harvard. His primary areas of scholarship are theological commentarial writings in the Sanskrit and Tamil traditions of Hindu India, and the developing field of comparative theology. He has also written on the Jesuit missionary tradition, particularly in India, and the dynamics of dialogue in the contemporary world. Clooney is the author of numerous articles and books. He is a Roman Catholic priest and a member of the Society of Jesus. In July 2010 he was elected a Fellow of the British Academy.

Rick Devin—Understanding from the Very Core

Given a set of tangible parameters such as a blank canvas, paints and brushes, I am usually able to find a way to convey my passion and/or meaning for an idea, esoteric or otherwise. This gives me meaning in a brief moment in my life. However, when actually confronted by an all-encompassing entity that has lurked in my mind since childhood, I tend to be sporadic in my thought process. One moment hedonistic, another guilty, another scared yet another of total worthlessness. These weigh upon my mind, while my body is being assaulted by drugs, radiation and ultimately surgery. I draw from the past, both good and bad moments trying to distill a sense of balance, while trying to keep the best in front of me. This is always a struggle, as the ugly stuff always seems to position itself in the foreground.

Perhaps felt but unsaid feelings from loved ones give me myriad reasons to rise above the malevolent malady called cancer. The meaning and fulfillment comes from the very core of who "we" are. They give, I take and give back. They take, I give and take back. Each time I'm gaining another brief moment of being. I'm here for them, but have to be here for myself to find a way that propels me forward in this constant pursuit of meaning and living. It's layer upon layer upon layer which sometimes solidifies and/or other times just sloughs off, only to be built up again, creating another direction in the constant search.

Rick Devin has been plying his craft and defining his art for over forty years. He was born in Pittsburgh. After a brief time in advertising and illustration, he established himself as a freelance artist. He accompanied his wife and two sons to Haiti several times, while she pursued her doctorate and he taught basic art. He has served on the local town council and school committee and was an art festival director for ten years. He opened a small gallery/studio in his home over twenty years ago and lives with his wife in Hope Valley, Rhode Island.

Adeline DiRocco—"The Circle of Life"

You are born to this world.
Soon you are a toddler and you know a whole new world.
Life is wonderful.
You learn new experiences every day.
You go to school and make friends outside your home.
Soon you become a teenager and life becomes complicated and
    fearful because you don't know the future.
You finally start dating and meet your spouse,
then you marry.
You have a new family of your own.
Life is so different, sometimes joyous, and sometimes very trying.
Your children become adults and soon they leave and marry.
Life is passing so fast in your later years.
You face illness and many disappointments.
What could you have done differently?
You begin to recall your life and pray your last days are peaceful
    and content.
The circle of life is completed.
When shall you leave this life?

Adeline DiRocco was born in the middle of the Roaring Twenties surrounded by her 11 siblings in Providence, RI. She and her husband, Alfred, raised their family together in a quaint yellow house in Johnston, RI. She is patient, kind, and is a role model of perseverance. When asked by her granddaughter what she wanted her biography to say, Adeline exclaimed, "Tell them all to enjoy life!"

Richard Giannone–The Mind Lies, the Body Tells the Truth

At the age of thirty-three in 1968, I contracted hepatitis B that fulminated into a coma and four-month hospitalization (with pneumonia) and year-long recovery. I was dark yellow, so was my urine, though my stools were white. Bile does that reverse bodily trick. I was near death. I didn't know that death was imminent. I brought my entire biography to the condition, which is to say I was fearful, denying, and stymied. It never occurred to seek meaning. Liver disease was the meaning, that and nothing more. I understood that I depended on the medical staff and friends who came to visit the hospital. Mostly they brought silence and treats for which I had little appetite. After a while they had their lives to live. I had just the medical people.

I didn't look for meaning. Meaning came to me. It took two forms, emotional numbness and human relations. The incapacity for feeling and sensation prevented me from brooding, and happily, from indulging in self-sorrow. While aware that human relations were precarious, I recognized that people defined what faith I had.

I will certainly bring my entire biography to my dying. In that case, meaning and significance will probably seem extraneous. The mind lies. The body tells the truth, at least a truth, because it cannot lie. The body knows how to die. I know that I am putting more trust in flesh than it can hold. Still, I hope that I can let it guide me.

Richard Giannone is a 79-year-old professor of English who has taught at several universities and is still at it—now as an adjunct, the rank at which he began in 1958. He seems always to be at new beginnings. Richard and his partner Frank of 32 years are thinking of marriage to reduce taxes and facilitate transfer of their New York apartment. His new book Hidden: Gay Life, AIDS and Spiritual Desire came out in 2012.

B. L. Headtinkerwalla—Death-in-Life

The experience of a death, in the midst of life, is always individual, personal—and, usually, painful! Yet when notions of death, meaning, and life are examined more abstractly, or philosophically—extrapolating from the individual to the cosmic scale—the potential fluidity, or even reversibility, of familiar definitions becomes apparent surprisingly quickly. The early Christians could see all of "fallen" life as death; for Buddhists, all of conditioned existence, ultimately, is still some degree of bondage; Hindu metaphysics classifies all of phenomenal existence itself as Maya (life itself as delusion or illusion or misperception). In the early 1950s, Meher Baba (1894–1969) succinctly expressed, along these lines, that:

> Unless and until ignorance is removed and Knowledge is gained—the Knowledge whereby the Divine Life is experienced and lived—everything pertaining to the Spiritual seems paradoxical. God, whom we do not see, we say is real; and the world, that we do see, we say is false. In experience what exists for us does not really exist; and what does not exist for us, really exists.
>
> We must lose ourselves in order to find ourselves: Thus loss itself is gain. We must die to self to live in God: Thus death means Life.

Surely, though, the lived meaning of such reversals is not gained through platitudes, or by New Age "positive thinking" ideologies, or through any repression or denial of death (as commonly defined). One still suffers deaths even as they are not, and cannot, be the real gauge of life.

B. L. Headtinkerwalla is the editor of the 2005 pamphlet William Stringfellow's Circus: "The Idea of Society as a Circus" (1966) & several circus-related excerpts from Stringfellow's other writings.

Colby Hopkins—Whose Life Did I Make Better

How does one change the world? I mean, if we are to find fulfillment facing death, we must ask ourselves "what do I hope to accomplish in my lifetime?" I dream of making the world a better place.

This does not minimize the value my family and friends contribute to my life. I am truly blessed. My mother, sister, brother (nieces and nephews) and I have incredible relationships; most people I know don't have friends as close as my cousins and I; my closest friends recognize me as I am and offer me countless shared and joyful experiences; and I held out long enough to find the perfect partner—one that completes, understands, and invigorates me. They nourish my life and elate me.

But what do I give back? I do not seek notoriety, recognition, or awards. When I look back at my life I want to have answers to the question "whose lives did I make better?" I want to be able to close my eyes and picture their faces. I want to see their smiles and know that I, at least in some small way, contributed to those smiles. I want to know I made their lives better.

Colby Hopkins is a researcher, writer, and activist who fervently pursues a better, more humane world. He has spent his life studying history, political science, economics, international relations, human rights, and social justice. He was an organizer with Occupy Wall Street and the West Harlem 99% in New York from September 2011 until August of 2012 when he moved to Palestine with his partner to teach English. He loves music and art. He holds teaching degrees in several martial arts styles. In 2013, he published his first book, Another World IS Possible: Freedom, Economic Truth, and Creating a Society of Humanness (2013).

Alfred G. Killilea–We Are One Vast, Dysfunctional Family

My life has been shaped and enriched by countless people I never knew. I find significance in life in being a part of this immense web, this interconnected community. Death does not cancel what we receive and what we give. In fact, death pushes us to realize and appreciate the power that all of us have to affect the lives of others.

Death has not been a stranger to me. My father died when I was twelve and twenty five years ago at the age of 16 my precious daughter, Mari, was snatched casually and cruelly by death. I could not have loved two people more and I continue to feel the wounds of their loss, and the loss of many others dear to me. But their spirits are within me. They are a part of me, as, after we die, each of us will be a part of those we love, and even of those whom we have touched and do not know.

We do not need a God or an afterlife to affirm that life is not mocked by death. Pain and suffering are an intimate part of everyone's existence, especially when brutes like Hitler seek importance by doling out death to innocents. But those harsh realities do not negate the fact that we all have the gift and opportunity to enhance the lives of one another and that we will always be a part of this vast human family.

Alfred G. Killilea graduated from the University of Notre Dame and received his Ph.D. in political science from the University of Chicago. Before his recent retirement, he taught political theory for 43 years at the University of Rhode Island. He regularly leads workshops on ethics for public officials. He is the author of THE POLITICS OF BEING MORTAL and recently edited CONFRONTING DEATH: COLLEGE STUDENTS ON THE COMMUNITY OF MORTALS (www.confrontingdeath.com) He most enjoys teaching students and playing basketball with his peers and grandchildren. He now serves as a University Ombudsman at the University of Rhode Island.

Susan Matarese—Death and Our Interconnectedness with All Living Things

If one knows that what is born will end in death, then there will be love. Buddha.

Cultivating an awareness of death is at the same time cultivating an awareness of life. To me, death is a great mystery. Contemplating the death of loved ones as well as my own death brings sadness but also acceptance. In fact, I think that consciousness of death has helped me to live more mindfully, to focus on the present rather than dwelling on the past or worrying about the future.

The experience of vulnerability that comes with thinking about death has made me more compassionate. It has also made me grateful for the life I have. It puts many of the vexations and challenges of daily living in perspective. It's hard to take things quite so seriously in the face of the inevitability of death. Paradoxically, an awareness of death also amplifies the joys of relationships with family, friends, students and special animals, the fulfillment that comes through work well done and the contentment I feel while engaging in activities like singing, riding, hiking and gardening.

In another way, the inevitability of human mortality is strangely comforting. Death is the great democrat who comes to all of us, rich and poor, good and evil, powerful and weak. This recognition reinforces my sense of belonging and interconnectedness with all living things. In the end, it is kindness, authenticity, love, humor and grace that really matter.

Susan Matarese is a Professor of Political Science at the University of Louisville where she teaches courses in Political Theory, Comparative Government and Utopian Studies. She has won numerous awards for distinguished teaching including the prestigious Red Apple Award. Dr. Matarese grew up near Boston, Massachusetts and earned her Ph.D. from the University of Minnesota in 1979. She came to Louisville the same year. She is the author of the book, <u>American Foreign Policy and the Utopian Imagination</u> that was published by the University of Massachusetts Press. She has also authored dozens of articles on the subject of American utopias and is currently writing a book on the health practices of the Shakers. Dr. Matarese lives in Shelbyville with her husband Dr. Paul Salmon.

Katherine E. McAllister—The Moments In-between

When thunder tears through my dreams in the twilight hour I fall gently into a deeper place that feels like soul. I am half there and half here in clean white sheets softened by the sleep of generations. Here, death and life stand the same distance from me, close. They are my composition, revealing themselves in simultaneous cycles with faces disguised as one another.

It is in moments in between while life and death exchange breath within us that there are bursts of brightness and purpose and meaning. There is no essential lasting fulfillment, no one final meaning, only the exploration of a lifetime inside us for what is at once elusive and potent. My grandmother calls, to thank me for a package. I want to talk to her about death, to tell her that I will miss her like I have never missed anyone in my whole life, to tell her that I love her. Instead both of our voices pitch higher because we might cry if one of us utters a word any closer to the truth. THIS is death and life. Without love to animate it, there is nothing but motion. I feel fulfillment when my heart strains and threatens to burst for that I have loved and lost. I experience, in rhythm, life and death. No matter the potency of pain, to have truly loved, one cannot lose.

The cycle moves and night falls. I think now that life and death are mere opinions because they exist at once in all. On this night, I find meaning in a laborious town meeting that yields the approval of a community fundraiser. I am fulfilled for a moment as I step off into the warm night, heat lightning in the distance and the weighted stillness hugs me close with the intimacy of a lover dancing in a transparent fog.

From the blacks and blues and outline of trees sounds the cacophony of crickets and the whir of cicadas. A piano caresses my ears from the crackling radio. Thunder again, in the distance, and here are the moments in between.

Katie McAllister is a new mother to a baby girl, partner to an amazing man, and life-long lover of words and expression. Fourteen months have passed since the moments that inspired this piece, and to re-read it unleashes a flood of new responses from a heart that is broken open daily. One day while pregnant with her daughter and driving through North Kingstown, RI, where they reside, she wondered about her child's purpose in this world. A sudden feeling overwhelmed her as she received a response- "to love." She believes that although life can be a great struggle to us all, we will endure so long as we remember to always choose love.

Richard McIntyre–Combatting Appalling Moral Amnesia

I am descended from Irish immigrants on both sides of my family.

These people left me the Catholic faith and a love of beer and "the craic," the Irish term meaning good conversation. My father, Allan McIntyre, saw much death as a young corpsman in the Pacific war. The event that stayed with him most was the summary execution of Japanese prisoners coming back from one of the battles. The American officers just did not want to be bothered with prisoners.

Allan was active in church, essentially the social action chairman of his parish. One day after a few beers, he told me he did not believe in the afterlife. He was active in the church because it was "the right thing to do." I did not understand this then.

When my children were born my first wife and I thought we should go to church "somewhere." We tried a local congregational church because it seemed less rigid and we had friends there. It was nice but did not feel right. Eventually we found a Catholic parish that we attended semi-regularly and I still do. I'm not always sure why.

Allan intuitively understood that the pursuit of the good life is the good life, and that this can only happen through definite practices within a community. Through reading Alasdair MacIntyre—a distant relative no doubt—I have learned about this and how one may draw together Aristotle, Aquinas and Marx to act in a world of appalling moral amnesia.

But this is not really an intellectual enterprise and I have learned more from my mother and second wife than from books. Katherine's faith, which I don't understand, has helped her to survive the death of many loved ones and to devote her time and energy to other people. My wife Deborah, who worked for years as a hospice nurse, responds to people with the kind of sympathy and generosity that Aristotle thought was at the heart of virtue, and which I hope someday to achieve myself.

Richard McIntyre is 57-years-old and lives in Wakefield, Rhode Island. He is married to Deborah Barber, has two children, three step children, five grandchildren (six any day), and two cats, Merry and Pippin. He is Professor of Economics and Political Science at the University of Rhode Island where he also teaches in the Master's program in Labor Relations and where he was Director of the Honors Program for many years.

Barnaby McLaughlin—Death Precedes Life

The question itself assumes a certain distance from death that only occurs from our constant disavowal of mortality. While death may not present us with a face to gaze upon, it is a constant in our lives. The fuels that power our machines, the animals (and plants) on our plates, the cells that flake off of our skin, they are all faceless death. In fact, our very existence is the result of an unknown number of species going extinct and we can push that even further and say that all life exists only because of death. The death of stars creates the very possibility for what we understand as life; therefore, we can say that death itself precedes life.

Why then do we only acknowledge death—or give death a face—when we are shown our own death? When only our own death possesses a face, meaning and fulfillment are an impossibility because death becomes annihilation—a return to nothingness. Only with the acknowledgement that death precedes life, that death creates the very possibility of life, is the specter of annihilation eliminated. Instead of a return to nothingness, it is a return to that which life comes from, death. Our bodies will continue to nourish and sustain the beings that come after us, just as the death of others sustained us during our lives. This is not only meaningful, but also incredibly powerful. To know that in my death is the power to create and sustain life itself.

Barnaby McLaughlin is an English Literature Ph.D. candidate at the University of Rhode Island. As avid animal lover and vegan, he has sought to focus his academic work on understanding why our representations of our fellow species in literature matter and how they help us understand ourselves. Barnaby has a passion for poodles and the Los Angeles Lakers. He also genuinely believes that all problems can be solved by consulting the works of Franz Kafka. Recently, Barnaby and his wife, Dianne, have been enjoying watching their first child, Lockhart, explore the world with a relentless curiosity and hysterical giggles.

Gerhard Müller–Each Death Is a Birth

My youthful sense of immortality was shattered in a childhood accident that almost killed me. A deep sense of gratitude for being alive slowly emerged from that experience. Out of it grew the awareness that our innermost core is untouchable by bodily injury or mental impairment. In contemporary academic discourse on consciousness this is called a delusion. The awareness of a spiritual reality has been reinforced by my life experience as a scientist, teacher, spouse, parent, and Baha'i. The fragility of life in this world raises existential questions with no simple answers. We all respond with a fantasy whether we admit it or not. The fantasy may be wrong but must do no harm if it is.

I see life as a process of consciousness and perception unfolding in stages. First the clock starts ticking, then space uncurls: we are born. The five senses grow sharper, then begin to fade. As we mature, if given the chance, our capability of perceiving spiritual reality is enhanced. The last veil is removed, or all veils at once, when our umbilical cord to physical reality snaps. Each death is a birth, every stage a classroom for the next. In embryonic stage we grow organs that are vital after birth. In this world we acquire spiritual attributes that equip us for what comes next. Learning to lead a moral life is one task. It includes reconciling thoughts, feelings, words, and actions. Handing over a better world to the next generation is another task.

Gerhard Müller was born in Switzerland. He teaches physics and conducts physics research at the University of Rhode Island. He finds it educational to have been living 30 years in a small country and 30 years in a big country. He is grateful to have been immersed in different languages. Gerhard and his wife Christine, a pianist and piano teacher, have one daughter, Martina, and two sons, Manuel and Michel. Every family member makes music.

Kuldip and Satwant Singh—Reconciling with Death

Death is the only certainty in life. It gets engraved in our being the day we are born. The only way to avoid death is not to be born and that's a bit too late for all of us. This renders the word death in the title above meaningless. So the real question is, "How do we find meaning and fulfillment in life?"

We believe that the real obstacle on this path is death itself. We treat death as something abstract that only happens to others; we avoid thinking about this anxiety-provoking fact. If we were to acknowledge our mortality, and remember it as we live our day-to-day lives, we would be better human beings and the world would be a better place for it.

How does one get past the fear of death? We believe one way is to contemplate about death—that it's real; it's going to happen to us and our loved ones one day. Death is a landmark in life, just like birth. This process of reconciliation with death has to begin rather early in life and not when one is looking at death in face. However, it's easier said than done for it takes persistent reflection and contemplation for years before this self-evident truth gets embedded in one's psyche at a conscious level. Once it happens, one becomes free and is willing to act on one's convictions and beliefs and find meaning and fulfillment in life.

It's easy to fool oneself about having made peace with death and dying. The real test comes when confronted with death. We recently faced this situation when my father-in-law got acutely sick. He was 89 and we had had discussions about life and death for the past several years. He expressed time and again that he was not afraid of dying, but at times adding "It's hard to imagine not being a part of this life, surrounded by children, grandchildren and great-grandchildren which makes it all so wonderful and enjoyable." Yet when the reality of acute illness with poor chance of meaningful recovery hit, as hard as it was on all of us, we did the right thing—accepted death with dignity in line with his wishes, over extended invasive and futile treatment that modern medicine has to offer. Fifteen years earlier, we faced a similar situation with my mother, who suffered a stroke. As it became clear that there would be no recovery, the discussion turned to "we hope she doesn't linger on" from "we hope she survives" within days. We do not believe that we would have gotten to these conclusions in a timely manner were it not for the fact of accepting death as a reality of life at a conscious level by all concerned.

As Steve Jobs stated in his commencement address to Stanford in 2005, "Remembering that I'll be dead soon is the most important tool I've ever encountered to help me make the big choices in life. Because almost everything—all external expectations, all pride, all fear of embarrassment or failure—these things just fall away in the face of death, leaving only what is truly important. Remembering that you are going to die is the best way I know to avoid the trap of thinking you have something to lose. You are already naked. There is no reason not to follow your heart."

Once one reaches this state, life has so much meaning and fulfillment to offer.

Kuldip and Satwant Singh are married and are both physicians practicing in Cincinnati, Ohio. Kuldip K Singh grew up and received most of his education, including medicine, in India with post graduate specialization in the States. She is wife, mother, and grandmother and practices psychiatry. Her roles in life have not only enhanced her understanding of human nature but also allowed her to help a lot of people to deal with the vagaries of life. She enjoys travel, reading and cooking. Her life and blood is her family and friends and she loves to meet new people. Satwant Singh grew up and studied medicine in India. He moved to the USA in 1970 and specialized in kidney diseases. Currently he is Professor of Medicine and Program Director at University of Cincinnati Medical Center in Cincinnati, OH. His passion is teaching and practicing medicine. He is a hands-on husband, father and grandfather. He is a people-person and has made several lifelong friends along the way. His hobbies are travel, music, and golf.

Ashley Stoehr–I Am Unafraid

Once upon a time I used to be a Catholic. Today, I am an atheist. I may be cliché, another biologist lost from faith's salvation; yet, I am unafraid. My matter has been and will be places, I cannot dream; the ultimate, personified beauty. My atoms burst from stars and walked the earth as dinosaurs; they climb cliffs, swim seas and have a future beyond me. Similarly, my consciousness will continue in the memories of those I have affected, preserving some slice of my mind-world relationship. Only at the surface is death physical doom and conscious separation, the agonizing pain of losing loved ones; for me, their matter is in the wind, their words in my memories. Their names will be lost in time, but I can carry their physical and mental portraits through generations leaving their genes and memories to "be" the future. I must live for them.

Everyone follows a path, and at some point individuals come to "know" their own personal truth. Mine is the circle of life through the revolution of atoms and the evolution of thoughts; to become no more than a physical or conscious imprint in something somewhere. Perhaps, someday some atomic part of me will toast memories at the end of the universe. My fulfillment in life stems from a lack of fear or concern for an epilogue, only the present storyline matters. There is no happily ever after, merely the journey's final drink, but that last sip will be glorious.

Ashley Stoehr (B.S. Marine Biology, B.A. Political Science), 24, is a dedicated life-student currently, and for the foreseeable future, pursuing a doctoral degree in Biomedical Engineering and Biotechnology with a concentration in Marine Physiology. As a native New Englander she is all about the sun and vitamin D, enjoying numerous outdoor, non-sea level sports like rock climbing and scuba diving; although in a pinch the physiological responses to yoga are also incredible. Ashley loves stories; and is constantly reminding herself to "enjoy the moment, the current plot, because in two weeks it will be a memory."

Judith Stokes–I Know How to Live My Life Well

Wisdom admits no struggle with death at my age. It may be hubris on my part to claim wisdom, but the first half of my life is certainly over. Age has already taken some of my energy. I cannot improve on most of my accomplishments, and some goals are no longer available to me. There is no wise alternative to acceptance. During very dark nights in the winter, I may succumb to the mid-life struggle again, but every year it becomes easier to remember that the second half of life is a bonus.

Maturity has brought me faith, not in god or heaven or kismet, but in life and death as two sides of one coin. Agnostic my entire adult life, I have found truths in the Exodus that others may have found in the Iliad or the Gita. To disbelieve any sacred text seems to me to deny them all. Such chutzpah to pick and choose among gods! In times of trouble, however, my lack of faith was often a painful void. When my father died, and many people assured me that he was in a better place, I wept in envy of their certainty.

Now I am certain, not that I pray to the right god, only that I know how to live my life well. When I die, even if my dad is not there waiting for me on the other side, I will be satisfied. Death will be what death will be.

Judith Stokes is a 63-year-old academic librarian. The most mystical experience of her life was having children and loving them and their father together. The most enduring is reading books and sharing thoughts with other readers. The most mundane is constructing paths toward knowledge through accumulations of information, whether the collections in libraries, the chaos that is the Web, or the art in a well-written story. The values of librarianship have helped sustain her most lasting friendships.

Michael Vocino—Meaning and Improving the Human Condition

Most of us avoid the subject of death at all costs. We suppress and avoid the knowledge that we will all eventually die and that death is permanent. We see the denial in the orthodoxies of all the world's religions, whether the avoidance is defined as "heaven," "reincarnation," or something else. In one form or another, most cultures of the world have a value system that includes the belief that although physical death is a solid reality, in some way or another, we, as individuals, will live on after the death of our current physical form. Whether we believe that or not, all of us believe that life is driven by death and that we need to find meaning for our lives.

In the face of death, most theologians and philosophers also make it clear that we should live the "good life", all the while interacting well with others. Their methods may be different, but whether it be Jesus, Muhammad, Moses, Buddha, Marx or another prophet/philosopher, our lives only have importance inasmuch as they help the human condition progress and that we as individuals, communities, or societies act and live to insure that positive progression.

Knowing that we will eventually end, that we will all die, makes it imperative—because of our nature—that we create meaning for our lives. Whether politics, culture, the pursuit of knowledge, religion or whatever, we all understand that the meaning we seek and create should contribute in some way to the positive progress of the human condition and that this should be the central motivation of our lives in the face of eventual, certain death.

Michael Vocino is a former Dean of Libraries at the University of Rhode Island. He has taught film and political science and is currently the University Gifts Librarian. At the end of each academic year, like Monet (to whom he bears a resemblance), he walks into his garden until the end of July and comes out only to travel to his small apartment near the beaches of the Gargano Peninsula for 'Ferragosto.' During the academic year, as he approaches retirement, he catalogs gift books, reads, watches films and television incessantly, and writes short stories. He's also the full-time servant of his cockapoo, Joe, the alpha-male in their relationship.

Steven Williamson—Marx and Death

Someday I will pass from this world and those that knew me will pass as well. Everything I have written and everything I have done will be eaten away by relentless time, or will meld seamlessly into the material world of social production. The window I fixed today may remain unbroken for two hundred years, but no one will know who fixed it, just as I do not know who made it. In the middle of this great cycle of living, remembrance, and forgetting, there is one thing that will surely outlast me. The state, which has still not withered away, will keep a record of my life in the form of a number. Nine digits long, it is attached to the state's summation of my life. It tells the total I have earned each year, the amount I have paid to them, and perhaps one day the amount they will pay back. It is the summation of the value of all the hours I have sold. It is the exchange value of my life. Thinking of this I become nostalgic for times I've never known when no attempt was made to assign a number to a person, to a life. We worked, ate, lived, sang, mourned, and died like the innumerable sea birds and stars. Even now the innumerable dead from all the generations pile up behind us and perhaps will again in the future. Not quantity of life, but quality. Not exchange value, just use value.

Stephen Williamson is a teaching assistant and Ph.D. student in political science at the University of Connecticut, Storrs. His primary interests are comparative politics (Latin America), political theory and political psychology. He did his undergraduate work at St. John's College (MD).

CHAPTER 7

Death And The Tragedy Of Life

"Our dead are never dead to us, until we have forgotten them."
—George Eliot

Frank Annunziato–Death As Emptiness

Just as Butterfly McQueen's Prissy didn't know "nothin bout birthin babies," I sure don't know "nothin" about death and dying. I am not a philosopher and to quote one of my daughters, "deep thinking gives me headaches." My first experience with death happened when I was almost five years old and my beloved grandmother went to the hospital and never came home. Death, from that point on, meant emptiness to me and I experience that same feeling whenever someone I love dies. "We'll never see her again," my mother cried at the death of her mother. I learned then that the dead exist only as memories for the living.

When I first tried to write something about death, I became fixated on one scene. I was back working in New York City. It was St. Patrick's Day and I was waiting to cross Fifth Avenue to get to my office on 43rd Street, nearer to Sixth Avenue. The line of marchers, the barricades, and the hundreds of policemen protecting the parade allowed no pedestrian to get to the west side of Fifth Avenue. While it was wonderful experiencing the sounds and sights of New York's biggest parade, I had to get across. What did this metaphor mean? On the one hand, the marchers symbolized death because they were heading inevitably to the same place. On the other hand, crossing Fifth Avenue represented death because everyone must experience it alone. Either interpretation results in the same conclusion: death will come, as Shakespeare attributed to Julius Caesar, "when it will come."

I don't fear death, but if I had a choice, I would want to spend as much time as possible watching or marching in the parade.

Frank Annunziato holds a Ph.D. from the University of Connecticut and is a long-time labor organizer. He is currently the Executive Director of the University of Rhode Island Chapter of the American Association of University Professors. His life has changed considerably—and for the better—since the birth of his fraternal twin grandsons last year.

Geraldine Barry—I Have No Answer to Death

Most of the time I don't think I can possibly be close to dealing with "the face of death",

but at other times (Whose hands are these? Who is that in my mirror?) it does occupy my thoughts considerably.

Mostly I think of how lucky I have been and why have I been so lucky? There is no answer and I think that is what I accept...there is no answer and there is nothing beyond what we have here. I so enjoy my family and my life that I want it to keep going on and on and that is what brings me my fulfillment every day. To think of leaving this is what is disconcerting.

Now I am in my 66th year and I still wake up eager for my first cup of tea and some reading time before our home starts bustling. Our teen girls, two of our four sons, my husband and I comprise this household right now. This week-end another son and a friend will join us from N.Y. All are healthy... and here. When I was 15, my mother died, suddenly to us (6 kids between the ages of 11 and 18). This has been the defining event of my life. When Jack and I married and began our life with our kids is when I started on my path to becoming who I am today...a person who values what I have.

Danielle Dirocco—Dismantled by Alzheimer's

A short time ago, my grandfather passed away. While he was always a regular part of my life as a child, we were never truly close to each other. Still, he was the first person in my life to pass away gradually, and before my eyes. I visited him and my grandmother numerous times as he slowly but persistently faded from being a real person to a shell of a human being. This is the way Alzheimer's dismantles a person—One tiny little bit at a time. Only a couple of years ago, I asked my grandfather to tell me about his experiences in World War II. I can still see the pained expression on his face as he dug into his memory to share his thoughts with me and, to his dismay, came back empty handed. I reassured him that day that it was okay, that everything was going to be okay in much the same way I quietly spoke to him on the night he died. His fingers that night were so deep a purple that you could have sworn he had recently voted in a Middle Eastern country, or that in his final days he had begun spinning silk dyed with cochineal or indigo to pass the time.

I wouldn't presume to say he was a great man; to the contrary, if I am to believe what I've been told, he was a simple man with many flaws. However, he was a man nonetheless, and it was an honor to be in his presence as he lived his last hours here on earth. Sometimes, you unexpectedly learn what is truly important when you least anticipate it. Who knew that that one hour of my life would have such a profound impact on my understanding and appreciation of meaning in life?

Danielle hails from the University of Rhode Island, where she earned her undergraduate degree in Secondary Education and History in 2009 and her MA in Political Science in 2013. She is currently the Executive Director of Graduate Assistants United, the graduate student employee union for the University of Rhode Island. Union activist by day, wife and mother by night, Danielle spends her leisure time collecting sea glass, basement trolls, and random bits of trivia while defending her apples and cheese from the world's grumpiest and most lovable cat, Mollie.

Paul Forte—Death Is Certain to All

"Death, as the Psalmist saith, is certain to all; all shall die."
—Shakespeare

Thoughtful answers to this question might reveal something of the resilience, even nobility of the human spirit, although those of us not facing the prospect of imminent death can only imagine what our responses would be under those circumstances. As it has been said: "Nothing focuses the mind like death." So the essence of the question is this: With the end in sight, would this focus expunge any possibility of a qualitative life in the time remaining? In other words, would the shadow of death eclipse one's life and make meaning and fulfillment seem futile, purposeless? This much is clear. And yet, given the inevitability of death the very question of finding meaning and fulfillment in its presence seems to hint at the tragic. If facing imminent death makes finding meaning and fulfillment somehow more elusive, perhaps the dying person has failed to realize these things while living. Such a person may then be forced to question how genuine one's life has been; how true they have been to their own dreams and aspirations. Whatever our proximity to death, one thing is certain: we will all cross its threshold and this passing is an integral part of life. Whether we die tomorrow or many years from now, death is, or at least should be, no impediment to lasting meaning and fulfillment in one's life. Tragedy arises when the full weight of eternity awakens a person to his or her lifelong denial of their human potential. Sadly, this is only revealed at the end of a life if and when the central question of meaning and fulfillment comes to the fore.

Sixty-six-year-old Paul Forte is a nationally recognized visual artist who also writes essays. A Vietnam veteran who came of age during the turmoil of the 1960's, he experienced the underside of life, including homelessness and substance abuse, and yet he never lost a sense of self or purpose. This experience has lent his work as both an artist and a writer a poignant and reflective quality. A man of simple tastes, Forte believes that life is best savored during those precious, quiet moments that somehow transcend the cacophony of our lives.

Joyce Goggin—In the Cards

When Wild Bill Hickok was murdered on August 2, 1876, in Deadwood, South Dakota, he held two-pair—aces and eights— and the queen of clubs. This combination is known as a "Dead Man's Hand" and, in spite of the gruesome associations, this hand holds out hope, not just of a full house, but also of fulfillment and evolving possibilities in the face of death.

A gamble can go two ways. It may end in tremendous loss and even death, or hitting the jackpot. Even for those who lose, gambling imparts fleeting sovereignty—knowing, for one brief moment what it is to have money to burn. Gambling is known as "edge work" because of its likeness to dancing over sublime vistas, and whistling past the multiple abysses of a landscape that culminates in a distant and vertiginous vanishing point.

Tottering on the brink of success or devastation is referred to as a "pathology of becoming", always waiting on the blind turn of a card. But while gambling may be pathological, in individuals or in markets, there is virtue in risk-taking and accepting the vicissitudes of chance. Against the certainty of death, nothing relieves monotony like the swoon of a chance encounter, a big loss or win, or a random event that stands out in a chaotic world. Gambling is not an answer, nor does it offer certainty—quite the contrary. Yet a wager heroically accepted may open a window onto meaning and fulfillment when life abuts in dead ends.

Joyce Goggin is a senior lecturer in literature at the University of Amsterdam, where she also teaches film and media. She has published widely on gambling and finance in literature, painting, film, TV, and computer games. She is currently researching and writing on casino culture, Las Vegasization and public debt, gamification and the entertainment industries.

Amar Lahiri—The Brutality of Death for Religion

We see death all around us and most of what we see of unnatural death is caused by religion. What especially brings home the meaning of death for me is the senseless slaughter of innocents, particularly children. Many times such brutality is done in the name of religion. We see it in Palestine, we see it in Northern Ireland, we see it in India, and we see it in Pakistan just to name a few of the most recent wars waged in the name of "faith." Our approach to humanity should be changed. We should not be focused on gods, but rather on the real problems of hunger, lack of housing, inadequate education and the like. The only way we can do that is to stop stressing our own achievements that bring us prosperity, wealth or personal recognition. Rather than continuing to wage wars where innocents die or are deliberately killed, we should guard against all forces, especially religious faiths that use brutality to advance their causes.

These brutal, premature deaths of children and other innocents are never justifiable. Death is inevitable as we see with the death of our parents and our other loved ones. It eventually comes for us too and we should do our work, whatever that be, until it does. More importantly, however, as we wish for a natural death for ourselves, we should also work to make sure that all unnatural deaths caused by war and other forms of brutality are erased from the human experience. As I wait for my own death, I will continue to work in my chosen field and I will continue to talk against unnatural deaths caused by war and other forms of human brutality.

Amar Lahiri is a professor at the University of Rhode Island where he is the longtime Head of Cataloging. He travels each year with his wife to visit family and friends in India and frequently visits his grandchildren in New York City. He has two daughters. One is a Pulitzer Prize winning fiction author and the other is a professor of political science. A film was made of one of his daughter's books, The Namesake, and he and his wife appeared as extras in one of the scenes. Though well into his eighties, he still works everyday and shows little sign of slowing down.

Lisa Libera—Death Swallows Everything You Love

I was raised Catholic, and truly believed it for a time. I believed hook, line, and sinker; I believed it all.

But I was curious and well read, even at an early age; I devoured books and especially loved mythology and mysteries.

I first saw my own death on the toilet, when I suddenly realized that I was going to end. I recall rushing to my room and hiding in my bed, covered in pillows and blankets and cowering in my nightmare-recovery pose.

My second death insight was at an amusement park. We were waiting in line for a ride, my family and extended family, and I suddenly realized that everyone I was with was going to die either in my lifetime, or it was going to be me first.

There was a certain era of morbidity after that. Lots of horror novels consumed.

And then my younger brother died suddenly at age 21. Theory became my workroom.

Death is like an ocean that swallows everything you love eventually. Overwhelming as it may be, the waves of time shape and carve out an artifact, and it is only finished when we die.

I look at life as a journey to that ocean, and know that my friends will be scattered about me on the beach when we are gone.

Lisa Libera is a musician living in a paralegal's body in the Boston Metro Area. She is often susceptible to random acts of writing and photography. She is currently a member of Muy Cansado and The Easy Reasons, performing on bass and vocals.

Marlene Malik—Death is Unfair
and a Complete Waste of Time

In the face of certain death, I understand that the moment of death is the "final kick in the ass" of life. Do I think it is unfair that in the end we die? Yes. After spending a lifetime doing my best and learning about the world around me it seems a complete waste of time and energy to end up dead, burned and ashes scattered. I won't go willingly into that great night. But, can I spend my life railing against the inevitable? Well I suppose I could but I choose to put that unfairness aside and live.

Because of my greed for life I want as much of it as possible. Everyday is a (here comes the cliché) gift to me. Not given to me by God. I am an avid and convinced atheist. Religion is foolish. It offers an afterlife which is comforting to some but not to me. I can deal with the fact that I live for a limited time and then I will die. In fact, a well lived life is not a gift that is given but one we can all take.

It is not difficult to find meaning and fulfillment in life. I truly believe that the cliché about "stopping to smell the roses and enjoy each and every day" has been a standard for my life. Raised as a foster child, when I was young I could always hope for the future no matter how difficult life presented itself. As I got older I could see the rewards for having lived through my struggles. The rewards are there every day through meaningful work, friends, family and the enjoyment of nature. I have tried to pass that onto my children and grandchildren, knowing full well that they must come to this themselves. I really believe each day lived well is part of doing the best I can do. But, of course I must ask the question why do the best I can do if indeed, my final reward will be the "kick in the ass." A valid question. However, given the choice, and we all have choices to live well or not to, for me it seems obvious. I have a certain amount of time and I can spend that time unhappy, complaining, selfish, greedy, angry and always wanting more. I have seen folks like that and some achieve their goals of wealth, success and whatever. But, I have also seen folks with those feelings unhappy, disappointed and worse than that, with regrets.

I want to live my life with no regrets. On some level who

cares—out is out. So why should it matter? I guess I want to leave this world having lived well. Having overcome difficulties, having been able to deal with adversity and still having enjoyed each day. Seeing goodness in everyone and having lived as good a life as possible remains a goal and until the last moment/breath of my life I intend to work toward that goal.

Does that sound a little "Pollyanna?" Yes. Is it realistic? Yes. Idealistic? Yes. Attainable? Yes.

Marlene Malik is 74. Recently retired from teaching sculpture at Brown University, she now spends her time with her family of 3 children and 7 grandchildren and working in a completely new field. She is a volunteer for CASA (Court Appointed Special Advocate) for children through the family court system in RI. These are children that have been neglected or abused as determined by the court. She continues to make art but less strenuous stuff. Digital photography. She and her husband live in Kingston, RI but travel as much as possible.

Michael McElroy—It's Pretty Damned Depressing

I'd like to believe that I will live forever. But of course I will die, and so will those I love. It's pretty damned depressing.

Frankly, death scares the shit out of me.

I guess there really are only two sensible options. Either there is some form of afterlife or there is nothingness.

If there is an afterlife, none of us knows what form it will take, and there is nothing we can do to change that.

If there is only nothingness, there is nothing to worry about because we will not have any awareness.

So intellectually I know there is nothing to be afraid of because everyone is going to die and without any knowledge of whether there is anything "on the other side."

Yet emotionally I remain scared shitless. Which I guess only shows that it is impossible to approach death intellectually. I think this is why religions hold so much appeal. Most religions assure us of some form of afterlife in which we are rewarded for our good deeds. That is emotionally satisfying.

How I find meaning and fulfillment in life in the face of certain death? For me, I do my best to ignore the fact that I will die. I bury myself in work, family, exercise, books, movies, and baseball. I enjoy being a grandparent and relating to my grown children as adults.

And, of course, I will as always worship at the altar of baseball and Fenway Park, which will live forever.

Mike McElroy has been a lawyer and a husband for 37 years, a father for 33 years, and a grandfather for 3 years. His passions include daily exercise, his kids and grandkids, the Boston Red Sox, the New England Patriots, good books, independent and foreign films, anything truly original and his beautiful wife, Christine. Mike is a partner in the Providence law firm of Schacht & McElroy. A graduate of URI, he earned his law degree from Boston University and his Masters in Taxation from Bryant University. He was the 2012-2013 President of the Rhode Island Bar Association.

Alison McMahan—We Can Only Live with Honor if We Claim Our Death

The question of death and morality leads me to the question of martyrdom and the media.

Islamic suicide bombers aim to be martyrs; they make video recordings before their deaths to guarantee themselves press. President Obama buried Osama bin Laden at sea, to avoid generating martyr-creating images.

I'm writing a book about Carlos Aponte, the Venezuelan revolutionary of the 1930s. Aponte was a savvy media manipulator; he once horsewhipped the chief propagandist for Gomez, the Venezuelan dictator, an act that mesmerized the press. Exiled from Venezuela, Aponte fought with Sandino in Nicaragua, then joined reformer Tony Guiteras' resistance to Fulgencio Batista's incipient dictatorship in Cuba. In 1935, Aponte, Guiteras, and sixteen others were gunned down by a force of over three hundred soldiers controlled by Batista.

These men died for an idea. An idea that took seed and grew: as martyrs they are heroes to both the Cuban and the Chavez regime, seen as forerunners to Castro and Che. Aponte's last words to Guiteras were: "Today is the day we die." Their aim was reform, their methods violent and media-savvy, and their acceptance of the reality of death, complete.

Our denial of death has made it too easy to become a death-dealing culture. If death has no meaning, then neither does killing. Carlos Aponte reminds us that we can only live with honor if we claim our death.

Alison McMahan is an award-winning screenwriter, author, and filmmaker. She is the president of Homunculus Productions. Her most recent documentary is Bare Hands and Wooden Limbs (2010) narrated by Sam Waterston. www. HomunculusProds.com Her book, Alice Guy Blaché, Lost Visionary of the Cinema, (Continuum 2002) was translated into Spanish by Plots Ediciones and has been optioned by the PIC agency to be made into a documentary film. A full list of her books and other publications can be found at www. AlisonMcMahan.com

Peter Nightingale—When I
Stopped Beating My Wife?

When I was about eighteen, I stumbled upon Bertrand Russell's *Why I Am Not a Christian*. Now, more than 45 years later, I still see myself standing in that corner bookstore, reading on the back flap:

"I believe that when I die I shall rot, and nothing of my ego will survive. I am not young and I love life. But I should scorn to shiver with terror at the thought of annihilation. Happiness is nonetheless true happiness because it must come to an end, nor do thought and love lose their value because they are not everlasting."

The experience of the moment and the memory so far of one's life determine its meaning and fulfillment; to both death is irrelevant. Indeed, as Epicurus wrote: "Death is nothing to us: when we exist, death is not; and when death exists, we are not." That, for me, once and for all settles this "question."

The quotation marks indicate that questions like "What is the meaning of life? " and "What is the purpose of the Universe? " only appear meaningful. In fact, they are perfect examples of what neo-positivists call pseudo-questions: syntactically correct sentences devoid of all but poetic meaning. Generations of secular and religious thinkers produced philosophy and mythology in response. In dealing with these questions, these scholars would have served mankind better if they would have admitted finding no meaning, rather than supplying meaningless and often self-serving answers.

Of course, none of this means that life is not worth living.

Peter Nightingale was born in 1947 and grew up in The Netherlands. He studied theoretical physics at the University of Amsterdam, where he also received his Ph.D. He moved to the US with his wife and three children in 1981; their youngest daughter was born in Seattle. He has taught physics at the University of Rhode Island since 1983. He sings and plays various string instruments. He joined the Raging Grannies, is active in the Occupy Movement and tries to leave behind a better, more just and peaceful, post-capitalist world for his children and grandchildren.

Rosa Maria Pegueros—The Hopes of a Devout Agnostic

I envy those whose faith is so strong that their response to the death of a loved one is to proclaim that they will be in a better place or that they are now meeting God. I have run the gamut from the intense faith of my youth, to the brash atheism of my college years; to a shrugging espousal of Marcus Aurelius' idea that having our loved ones remember us for having lived a noble life should be enough. Along the way, I converted from Catholicism to Judaism, more in the rejection of the sexism and gilded hierarchy of the Pope-dominated church and in the pursuit of a sensible way to live than for a way to face death.

My cool intellectual approach to life and death was shattered when my father died. Seeing him lying peacefully in his coffin, looking very much his sweet self, as if he would jump up at any moment, smiling and say, "Boo!" I suddenly realized that I could not imagine a future when I would never see him again. I understood the desire for an afterlife, the deep desire to be reunited with the ones we love. We had filled the pockets of his suit with candy, thinking that in heaven, finally, our diabetic father would enjoy the sweets that he craved.

I have come finally, to be a devout agnostic. I don't know if there is a God but I act as if there is. I read books on religion and engage in discussions about God because I can't let it alone. I don't have the faith to believe that there is an afterlife but I hope that there is. Religion, for me, has become a community with whom to join hands as we grope our way to the darkness.

Rosa Maria Pegueros is an Associate Professor of Latin American History, and Gender and Women's Studies at the University of Rhode Island. She is also a choral singer and writes about opera in her weekly blog http://operalovers-ri. blogspot.com/ She believes that the best antidotes to life's troubles are love, music, and dogs. Born in San Francisco, she lived in Los Angeles for twenty years before moving to Providence in 1993; now she cannot imagine living anywhere else. She lives with her partner, two dogs and two cats.

Lawrence E. Rothstein—Death and the Avoidance of Obligations

As I realize that my days are numbered and that the number of days grows smaller, I cherish greatly the time I have. With that realization, I become more and more focused on using my time to do things that make me feel good physically and mentally. Unfortunately for family, friends and colleagues, this often means not fulfilling obligations to others and taking better care of myself. It means doing more of the activities I enjoy and engaging in new endeavors that I have wanted to try for a long time. Day to day chores become more irksome. In my case this emphasizes a self-centeredness and a desire to avoid obligation that has always been a part of my makeup, but which, when time and energy seemed less limited, I was able to fight against with some success.

I am coming to terms with not being a star in any of my life activities—professional, athletic and personal. I do not expect to leave a lasting mark anywhere, but I am not disconsolate over this. I guess that is the fate of most of us. I am very grateful for having a very good life in terms of personal enjoyment and physical health and wish to continue and enhance those aspects of the good life for my remaining days. My fear of death is primarily a fear of dying, i.e. the declining quality of life and loss of enjoyment and health in the days leading up to death. As I have no strong belief in an after-life, I regret that death will mean that I will never again be able to enjoy the people I have liked and loved throughout my life.

Larry Rothstein is a 68-year-old professor and former civil rights and poverty law attorney currently on a half time phase-out to retirement in 2015. He has traveled extensively and lived all too briefly in Europe. He loves playing tennis and music, cooking, eating, biking and writing. He hopes that his family, including his wife and 19 and 21 year old children, do not suffer from his devotion of more and more time to those things and his growing impatience with anything that interferes with them.

Wallace Sillanpoa–The Sting of Death and Active Remembering

I t is a particularly difficult moment for me to address this theme since only one year ago I lost to a premature death my only nephew, son of a brother who also died young just two months shy of the birth of his one and only child. I am, and will continue to be, consumed by unrelenting pain at the loss; thus, too, my reverse, contradictory reaction to the poet's query, "Death, where is thy sting?"

Often I have sat before the bier of a loved one and while fixing my gaze on the motionless corpse, I have asked myself : "Yes, that is the body of the person I cared for, but where has that spark that gave movement and voice gone?" Despite adult rejection of childhood religious mythologies in terms of the Heaven-Hell paradigm, both the sting and my musings inevitably lead me to an aching and perhaps universal yearning for a someday reuniting with all those we have lost. Such reuniting, however, remains void of any material configuration since the "spark" of which I speak is, for me and many others, physiological and historical, and pretty linearly historical at that.

Active remembering keeps alive all those no longer here. I fight ferociously to hold on to my "spark" for as long as possible. The best way I know how to do so is through the riotous celebration of communal bread and song and indignant rant shared daily with those actively engaged in struggles for a better, a more just world, a socialist world, one in which perhaps I will be missed and remembered.

Wallace "Wally" Sillanpoa is a 67-year-old retired University of Rhode Island professor of Italian [his doctoral thesis examined aspects of Antonio Gramsci's PRISON NOTEBOOKS], a Gay man and socialist activist who continues to engage on all levels—political, moral, intellectual and cultural—in struggles for a world free of the perversities of racism, capitalism and U.S. imperialism. He and his Cuban partner just celebrated fifteen years of shared love of all that is just, kind and humane, together with their likewise shared hatred of all that is cruel, exploitative, unjust and morally irresponsible. He lives in Providence where he works for and dreams of socialism, both utopian and scientific.

Ellen Davis Sullivan—I Don't Find Any Large Meaning in Life

I don't find any large meaning in life, but I feel a sense of purpose when I help my family in ways no one else does. As an only child I visited my widowed father regularly while he was confined to a nursing home with Alzheimer's. I was able to share family stories and jokes with him, and once in awhile I coaxed a knowing smile from him when there wasn't much in his life he recognized. For thirty-one years I have been married to a man whose wife moved away, giving him custody of their pre-teen daughter. I take pride in my stepdaughter's accomplishments and sometimes wonder if my infertility was nature's way of assuring her of a mother substitute who would support and love her without competition.

I find fulfillment in activities I have chosen in retirement: writing and mediating. After a career as a lawyer, I trained in mediation and have resolved numerous lawsuits as a volunteer at a local court. I find it gratifying when parties settle their differences after I've listened to their stories. After writing for over twenty-five years, I've published two stories and have had several short plays produced. I belong to fiction and playwriting groups and I'm gratified to be part of a community of writers. I've lost some of the ambition that brought me to writing. I no longer seek to change my life through external rewards, though I would still like to publish a novel.

Ellen Davis Sullivan has been retired for 15 years after working as a corporate lawyer for 20 years and in private practice briefly after that. She volunteers as a mediator and finds that her best skills are in listening to people respectfully and helping them understand how to use the legal process to solve problems. She's had surprising success writing one-act plays after many years of writing mostly unpublished fiction. She writes that her greatest good fortune was meeting her husband and enjoying the 33 years they've spent together.

Jeff Swain—We Base Our Life on Chance

Life/Death. What's it all about? That's the biggest question isn't it? Are we an act of intentionality or an evolutionary hiccup? Are we the work made in the likeness of some divine creator or is our capacity for thought no different than the adaptive capability of the peppered moth, able to change its color to match the environment?

We get the answer in the end but to get it we pay for it with all we got. It's the cruelest of ironies isn't it? To have to live a life based on a premise we have no way of proving. Knowing for all our wanting and wishing that ultimately it's the toss of a coin, a line of binary code. It's either Yes or No; On or Off, and no amount of hoping, praying, and looking for signs can influence the outcome.

So that means we base our life on chance. To live is an act of faith but so is it to die. The difference is the former is a choice and the latter a foregone conclusion. At least that's what I tell myself each morning when I look into my shaving mirror and bring the razor to my throat.

William "Jeff" Swain is with Pennsylvania State University's Information Technology Services Department. He is a dedicated marathoner, blogger (http://jeffswain.net/) and is active on Twitter (@jeffswain). "I am not an expert on anything. Never was; never will be. I am a humble seeker. Happy in my role."

John Vocino—On Denial

"In the face of death, how do you find meaning and fulfillment in life?" Such an odd question to me. Although, maybe not so odd at this very moment. Here I am on a plane back to DC from a business trip. It just so happens that I share this small space with a number of colleagues and the cabin is swaying in turbulent air. If this plane goes down it does not mean we've lost the cure for cancer or AIDS. Civilization will still be able to travel in outer space. Our nation's economy will still muddle along; if the economy crashes it won't be because we crashed first.

But this unsettling moment, in which I have control over nothing externally will not be the time I question my purpose and value.

Maybe it's because I have lived in a form of denial that is greater than average. My wife and I are co-enablers in our denial, as we are closer to the expiration date than the born-on date. Some other common factors may also be contributing; being the youngest of our siblings, not having kids of our own, etc. It very well may be that my denial is rooted in my lifelong story arc of the late bloomer. Learned to walk late. Learned to talk late. Dating. Emotional intimacy. Formal education. Life lessons. Independence. Interdependence. Performance in my profession. Promotion. Responsibility. Respect.

And maybe its because I've spent most of my entire life -especially my adult one—in search of my best fit. And this search, these questions, came to me early on, before, throughout, and into the end of middle age. That area, skill or discipline where I am uniquely qualified. That thing a person gets straight A's for; even in the face of grudgingly accepting being the B student in my experience (although another, deeper part feels anger and frustration at those who have handed me the Bs as well as that side of me that was willing to accept that fate. The acceptance of that fate may be due to the other, optimistic part that has always held the belief that every experience is a lesson learned. That my best days are ahead. All the life lessons will pay dividends exponentially. Geometrically. This may be the rationalizations of a late bloomer. That, without this attitude, I would be sitting here hoping this sucker takes a right turn straight down and t-bones Graceland below.

Rational, logical inquiry. What keeps me aloft are learning and continual education—perchance that they will evolve into some level of wisdom some day. This is what navigates around the turbulence and sends me onto my next journey.

Maybe it's not even denial. It's that my focus is elsewhere. I'd rather hang out in Birdland than visit Graceland.

John Vocino was born, raised and educated in Kenosha, Wisconsin, and currently resides on Capitol Hill in Washington, D.C., with his wife, Diane Evans, and their 3 cats. He is a policy analyst for the federal government, and an expert on emergency management issues. Prior to joining the GAO, he served as a county planner and project administrator for St. Bernard Parish, Louisiana. He still plays baseball in the amateur leagues in Washington and has volunteered much time toward promoting an improved quality of life in the District of Columbia.

CHAPTER 8

Death And Appreciating Life

"As a well spent day brings happy sleep, so a
life well spent brings happy death."
—Leonardo da Vinci

Winifred Brownell—Waking Like Scrooge

eath is inevitable, except for those who believe spiritually in everlasting life; I am not troubled by its coming. Although I have had too many dear to me die or take their own lives, the knowledge that my life as I know it will end inspires me to savor the time I have and enables me to find fulfillment and meaning in the smallest of things and the briefest of moments. I love my family and friends and I enjoy my profession. I have had the pleasure of working in higher education to help students learn, acquire skills, and pursue their dreams. Education inspires me to leave the world better than I found it and use the time I have left to make that possible. Donating my time, talents, and funds to assist others creates possibilities and hope. Every morning I wake like Scrooge in Dickens' <u>A Christmas Carol</u> grateful that I have another day to enjoy and to make a difference. I am aware of the egregious challenges that some people must face due to dire poverty, war, clinical depression, serious physical illness and more and who may never experience the life so many of us have. Those working for peace, a sustainable quality of life, access to education, and improved health care have my deepest admiration for the noble work they do. As death comes nearer, I am less interested in acquiring material things than improving life for others and that is how I find fulfillment and meaning.

Winifred "Winnie" Brownell is Dean of Arts and Sciences at the University of Rhode Island and professor of Communication Studies in the Harrington School of Communication and Media. An avid traveler, in 1979, she was the first URI scholar to visit China. In 1974-75 she coordinated the URI Honors Colloquium on "Aging, Dying and Death" and in 1996, she co-coordinated the Colloquium on "Mortal Questions." She is a passionate supporter of the visual, cinematic, literary and performing arts.

David Cicilline—Choosing One's Own Way

While reflecting on the question of how to find meaning and fulfillment in life even in the face of death, I recalled the words of Viktor Frankl, the existentialist and Holocaust survivor, who wrote, "Everything can be taken from a man or a woman but one thing: the last of human freedoms is to choose one's attitude in any given set of circumstances, to choose one's own way."

Frankl maintained his own will to live even in the face of unimaginable horrors at the Theresienstadt concentration camp, while his family, friends, and possessions were taken from him one-by-one. Sooner or later, all of us will have to face down our own mortality. But while we know that our life will one day be taken from us, we must always decide for ourselves how to respond to this reality.

That's why, in my own life, I try to live each day to the fullest and embrace each new challenge that presents itself. Although tomorrow is promised to no one, we can still make the most of each moment we have.

David Cicilline was first elected mayor of the City of Providence, RI in 2002, and re-elected for a second term in office four years later in 2006. He was sworn in on January 5, 2011 as a Congressman for the Second RI district. He serves on the House Budget Committee and Foreign Affairs Committee. He has gained attention for his fights in Congress for common-sense policies to help get small businesses, manufacturers, families, and seniors through these challenging economic times. As one of the few openly Gay elected House members, he is also a member of the LGBT Equality Caucus.

Joseph Creedon–Befriending Death

There is a phrase that I have never understood though I hear it quite often. The phrase is "an untimely death." The reason I have difficulty with that phrase is that it implies that there is a reality that could be described as "a timely death." I have never heard anyone say "it was a timely death." I have heard folks say that a death was a blessing because the dying person's suffering was ended but I have never heard anyone say "a timely death."

Death is an intrusion on our illusion of immortality. We know that death exists but most of the time death is conveniently "out there." We can deal with death that stays "out there" but when death enters into our personal time and space we are always thrown off stride. Why? Death reminds us that we are not in charge. In spite of all of our planning, all of our efforts to control the events of our lives in the end we are not in charge.

As a priest it has been my privilege to walk the last stages of life with a wide variety of people—from the very young to the very old. I have buried people across a wide spectrum of the human condition. In the end, the experiences are similar. Those who fight death lose; those who struggle to befriend death win. Those who lose never fully grieve. Anger and disappointment rule their lives. Those who win grieve and heal and find meaning in their lives.

If we are to live life fully, we must be willing to embrace death as a frequently unwelcome but necessary part of life.

In March 1981, Bishop Louis E. Gelineau appointed Fr. Joseph Creedon as pastor of Christ the King Church, Kingston, where he served for 31 years before retiring from active ministry. Father Creedon now assists in local parishes and continues to serve on the board of directors of the International Catholic Stewardship Council, based in Washington, D.C. He also plans to write a book on stewardship, and has also been encouraged to start a blog on the Internet. Noted for his lively sermons, as well as a finely tuned sense of humor, Fr. Creedon now lives in Narragansett and still enjoys playing golf.

Harold B. Davis—Death and Accepting Limitations

From the moment a child becomes aware of death, finiteness is known, feared, and denied. Death becomes a symbol of finiteness, irretrievable loss, separation, and inertness. Physical death and emotional death are inevitably intertwined.

Facing one's own death differs from the painful experience of death of loved ones. What are the last moments of awareness for a person with a terminal illness? Unknowable.

Terror, which may be masked by various symptomatology, is experienced when one is diagnosed with a potentially terminal illness. This terror can only be tolerated briefly before its denial or its transformation by transcending acts which suggest a life after death. How one is remembered and by whom becomes more important. Time, personal relationships, and the pursuit of interests are reevaluated. One's legacy and life story needs to be communicated. Strikingly, aging and facing death help people accept their limitations and allow for emotional experiences that have been excluded or limited, such as greater intimacy.

Dylan Thomas wrote, "Do not go gentle into that sweet night… rage, rage against the dying of the light," and Swinburne wrote, "We thank with brief thanksgiving…that no life lives forever…that even the weariest river winds somewhere safe to sea." The former rages against death, the latter accepts it as a release. One persistently wavers between the two experiences of death: a desire to live fully in the face of death and the relief from the weariness of a terminal illness. At some point a person lets go of life.

Harold B. Davis, Ph.D. is a consultant at the New York University Postdoctoral Program in Psychotherapy and Psychoanalysis, faculty and supervisor at the Institute of Contemporary Psychotherapy, and in private practice in New York City. He has published a number of articles, presented papers at national and international conferences, and held offices, including being president, in professional organizations. His psychoanalytic interests include object relations theory, existential and phenomenological thinking, and the relationship between psychoanalysis and literary works. His interest in novels, particularly of the nineteenth and twentieth century, is exemplified by his paper, "Graham Greene and British Object Relations Theory."

Alejandro de Acosta—A Grip on Life That Sends Death Away

A few years ago, I was riding my bicycle fairly fast on a bright summer afternoon. It was a hot Texas summer day and, with the heat and the breeze, I felt alive, my pores receptive to the elements. There was some kind of sound—grackles or cicadas—in all, a "great blooming buzzing" constellation of impressions. I recalled one of La Fontaine's fables...

It is the fable about the poor wretch who, pained and suffering, wishes for death; but, when death arrives, he changes his mind, sending death away in a sovereign gesture that can only be called fabulous. It is as though, no matter how diminished, most of us will hang on to whatever life we have in the face of death. It's also that we are already doing that. We should not, at an imagined final moment, be said to be clinging if we are, in living, already grasping and grasped by a fullness of experience.

That was the lesson of the sudden death-orientation and death-disorientation of my impressions that day. There was such a great life-saturation to my experience that it seemed to be, in contrast with an imagined last shred of life, perfect. But at the same time I could not help but imagine any shred of life as perfect. This sense of saturation is the grip on life, which grips us in return. What we say is meaningful or fulfilling grows out of that fullness. I think it is possible to learn to experience life in that way; in so living I do not deny death, but I feel that it is possible to send death away.

Alejandro de Acosta is a teacher, writer, and translator—in no particular order. He has taught philosophy in a university setting and is constantly participating in informal study groups. He also enjoys reading out loud. He is currently putting the finishing touches on two books of essays. He has translated the poetry of Carlos Oquendo de Amat and Jorge Carrera Andrade from Spanish and is working on more translations from Spanish and French. He flirts with the idea of blogging but has never been able to convince himself to commit to it. Alejandro still lives in Austin, Texas.

Kristen Mae Hopkins—Spend Time in Laughter and Inspiration

Like so many other turning points, we have to make a conscious decision how we want to live, even in facing death. I'm a medical social worker, new to the hospice field, and I have patients who are facing their mortality.

I don't know what it's like to know that I am dying. I don't know for sure whether I'll be able to face death graciously. But, for now, I listen. I sit with my patients, and I let them teach me. I've heard patients urge me to be appreciative, to know that being right isn't important, and when faced with that terminal diagnosis, to realize there is nothing to do but accept it and move forward.

Recently, I have come to realize that I have spent way too much time grieving my past—mistakes I've made and those of others that have hurt me in some way. Similarly, I have tried so hard to plan and prepare for seemingly arbitrary aspects of my future. In living purposefully now, I hope to someday reflect back and know that I spent this life with the faces who made me laugh and the minds who inspired me. I hope that I always feel full in knowing I followed my own feet in my own quirky way, and while finding my own fulfillment that I spread a little happiness too.

As a child, Kristen was inquisitive and always giggling, and as a spirited 30-year-old, she mindfully keeps the same pace. Raised in "little" Rhode Island, her curiosity about the South led her to the rural mountains of Western North Carolina. The majority of her work has been in community outreach and advocacy, and she is passionate about her recent endeavors with hospice. Kristen says she feels most accomplished when she knows she has earned the respect of those she admires, and when she knows her love has helped lighten the heart of another.

Susan Klopfer–Follow Your Plan and Don't Let Others Mess with It

At 64, I moved to Ecuador. Before I left, I got sick while hell-bent on directing lives of family members.

It was a simple book of healing by the English homeopathic physician, Edward Bach, which brought better health, and new meaning to my life; Bach's writings showed me how to stay healthy while finding meaning and fulfillment in life.

Primarily, absolute freedom is our birthright, and we can only obtain this when we grant that liberty to every other living soul. If we spend our time telling others what to do, we limit them and we limit ourselves, mentally and physically. We may even encounter disease.

For the person who suffers at the hands of another, say a parent who "knows" the perfect career path for their child, Bach advises to "take courage; for it means that you have reached that stage of advancement when you are being taught to gain your freedom…"

Be captains of your souls, be masters of your fate. You came into this world "knowing what picture you have to paint." Your path was mapped and "all that remains to do is to put it into material form."

So, cut the apron strings and run!

Susan Klopfer retired at 64 to Cuenca, Ecuador and is the author of three civil rights books, including Who Killed Emmett Till?, The Emmett Till Book *and* Where Rebels Roost: Mississippi Civil Rights Revisited. *She wrote* Cash In On Diversity (How Getting Along With Others Pays Off). *She is an award-winning journalist (Branson Daily News) and has been an acquisitions and development editor for Prentice Hall. She is the author of a Book-of-the-Month Club alternate selection on computing and is a freelance writer and active blogger. Klopfer is a graduate of Hanover College in Communication and holds an MBA from Indiana Wesleyan University. She is currently working on a civil rights saga of the Mississippi Delta, pre-Civil War through 2012. You can read more at* http://ebooksfromsusan.com)

Ibrahim Abdul-Matin—Death : No One Is Very Good at It!

I was recently at a retreat on a hilltop farm in Vermont in the Mad River Valley. Surrounding us were green wooded hills. Yet just under 100 years before the land was almost totally stripped of its woods. Vermont, in the late1800's was practically cleared for sheep (wool) and timber. Now, there are incredible forests. The land looks renewed and refreshed. My lesson here was that you can heal scarred land.

It was here that I met Johnny, a rancher from the Pacific northwest. He shared with me this message from a Lakota elder:

"What of this life?" the elder was asked
He replied, "This life? This is just practice"
"What is the next life?"
"Oh—we don't know what that life is"
"How do we know it is just practice?"
"Because no one is very good at it."

In Islam, there is ancient wisdom that tells us we are travelers and strangers on this Earth. There are sign posts and historical texts which tell me what was before and what will come after but in both instances I have no idea. All I know, according to my faith, is that this life is a trial and a test. In the face of this I place a premium on the moments which aggregate to my whole life. I revel in a breath, a step in a right direction, a laugh, a beautiful encounter.

I find meaning and fulfillment in two things: One, that I can heal my scarred soul the same way that we can heal scarred land and, two, I revel in the mundane—it means that I am alive and that I still have chances to be better at this "practice".

Ibrahim Abdul-Matin is a Lead Consultant with The Frontier Project. He is the author of "Green Deen: What Islam Teaches About Protecting the Planet" and contributor to "All-American: 45 American Men on Being Muslim." He is a former sustainability policy advisor to New York Mayor Michael Bloomberg and a regular contributor on WNYC radio's nationally syndicated news show "The Takeaway."

Hugh D. McCracken—On Happiness and Aloneness

Whether you are writing an ethical will, a living will, your own will, have lost a loved one; or, you are putting your hand to the wheels of science or industry, or are working for a cause that you believe will change the world, or are fostering close relationships with your family and friends, crucial questions that you encounter about death are: "Am I alone?", "Do I matter?", and in face of the answers "How do I pursue happiness?"

In Spontaneous Happiness, Andrew Weil posits emotional well-being as a balanced state of emotional contentment, serenity, comfort, and resilience tailored to our times and our places in life. I answer death through spiritual meditation on aloneness and the uniqueness of my passage through time to understand my place on earth, and to positively impact "my time" by working towards goals outside of myself. By developing simplicity, patience and compassion, by calming the inevitable anxiety of being alone and one person on a planet of billions, I believe I gain perspective on myself and on death. I am etching my happiness through compassion, science, passionate teaching, writing, producing, and by pursuing an understanding of myself to become the change I seek in others. "He not busy being born is busy dying." sang Bob Dylan. Death is inevitable, and etching on the surface of time with my own happiness is one way to counter death's entropic fold.

> Knowing others is intelligence;
> knowing yourself is true wisdom.
> Mastering others is strength;
> mastering yourself is true power.
> If you realize that you have enough,
> you are truly rich.
> If you stay in the center
> and embrace death with your whole heart,
> you will endure forever.
> —Tao Te Ching (1988, Harper Row).

Hugh D. McCracken is a teacher and writer who pursues his passion for soccer, coaching children and teaching coaches in Rhode Island. In past lives Hugh taught at St. John's College in the Bahamas, pursued degrees at UCLA and earned a Ph.D. from the University of Wisconsin. Hugh has published research on decision making, memory, and on movement control strategies in children and adults. After work at Northeastern University, Hugh left academe for high technology and award-winning Information Architecture teams at Sun Microsystems that wrote and produced videos and books in print and on-line media. Hugh is focused on learning about coaching children's soccer with 11-14 year-olds, and he lives with his partner Karen in Rhode Island.

John F. Murphy IV—The Elderly as Teachers of Meaning and Fulfillment

In the literal face of death, most people are concerned with the timing and their comfort.

As a physician, I help people make these difficult decisions. It is mercifully straightforward when someone has either a very curable condition or a terminal illness. In the gray zone in between, individuals have a variety of preferences ranging from minimal evaluation and management to "do everything." I have noted that people are most at peace as they approach death when their medical wishes have been respected, their dignity preserved, and they have some control over when to pursue a comfortable and graceful transition.

Meaning and fulfillment are determined earlier in life, and I have gotten a lot of insight from talking with elderly people who as a group seem generally unconcerned with the concept of death. I have heard some sincerely comment "I have had a great life," referring to their cherished relationships with family and friends. I have realized that others spend most of their waking hours caring for chronically sick family members, soldiering on without complaint. Yet others are passionate about their career, working until they are forced to retire. I do not have to wonder about meaning and fulfillment in life; I am fortunate enough to encounter role models every day.

John F. Murphy IV, MD provides cardiology services for Rhode Island residents. He is currently affiliated with Kent County Hospital in Warwick, RI. He is a 1990 graduate of the Warren Alpert Medical School of Brown University. He is married with children.

Yvette Nachmias-Baeu—Not the Day to Die

Finding no reason to wait, death can be impatient and swift. Or it can be a tease, drawing out its purpose, taking its time simply to prove a point: that beyond removing you from life by ending it, death wants you to understand the difference. Death is a noun that becomes a verb, when you are in its grip. There may only be a few moments to come to a conclusion about what makes life so precious. When you have faced death head on, watched it take away people you love, life begins to mean a great deal. The distinction between the two is profound.

This understanding tempts you to bargain with it, test it out. You are willing to stick your neck out—possibly lose the bet. You try out your theory on a straight, empty road in the middle of nowhere staring straight ahead, you say under your breath: do it—just do it! Your foot presses the pedal gently at first as you find your courage. Now you commit, pressing down more firmly, the pedal hard against the floorboard. The engine whines and the car builds speed. At 130 mph you and the car are happy to have let loose. Consequences, considerations, obligations, have all vanished and in their place is pure sensation. Just as suddenly, you release your foot from the pedal. The car slows down. Apparently, you still cling to earth. You realize this is not the day that you will die, but you also know with certainty that you have truly been alive.

Yvette Nachmias Baeu has led an eclectic life, following her wide range of interests to where they led. She has, for example, been a psychiatric nurse, a working actress, an advertising producer at a major New York agency, a farmer in Rhode Island, and a creative entrepreneur. A founder of the South County Montessori School, she also administered a Masters of Arts in Teaching program at Brown University. In 1999, she contracted a rare autoimmune disease and, surviving it, volunteered as a health coach advisor for the International Pemphigus and Pemphigoid Foundation. Then, too, all the while, she's been writing essays and poems and is about to embark on fiction.

Daniel Novak–Death Becomes
Ally, Friend, Companion

Some days impossibly hard, other days a gentle breeze...always summer.

St. Paul: "Die daily"...Me, I die once every two days...shabby sitting...

Breviaries, worldviews, ways of dying...youth, the illusory immortality; anticipatory dying (fearfulness); chronological disintegration; psychological death (e.g. humiliation); existential residue—your dominant feeling in terminal states (panic, confusion, trust, joy—i.e. how you construe things right now); Buddhist mindful awareness moment to moment (said of Ryokan: "In ceremony after ceremony he died."); with each step dying into eternity and living in the Kingdom here and now a la St. Francis, Sri Ramana, or Thich Nhat Hanh (no concern with afterlife/afterlives)...

A growing sense of the nearness of death?—Well, yes and no. All chrono-systems falling apart gets more real, no denying. But really the occasion of rising, identical instructions for living and dying, that same constancy referred to in Zen Mind, Beginner's Mind. Greater urgency?—Yes, but "make haste, slowly." Complete Urgency. Death becomes Ally, Friend, Companion—versus Bergmanesque chess match. Living without remainder...but Maezumi-Roshi, "When she died, my mother left everything!"

Practical Matters? Yes, a growing sense of Trust and Feeling Supported, Guided, Loved. Moments become portals of grace when we have the right mind/heart/hat on. Directly, quietly ask, "What is the quality I most need to practice right now?" "What must I do next to live in the fellowship of all beings?" "Where is the point of greatest ache?" "Where is the hand of the Lord, right now?"

Intensive Practice? Always! Spiritual practice not a luxury, but like breathing, like the ability to smile...Pervading Practice? Amidst our diligence/dithering, what mood descends? No control. Faithfulness. Reverence. Being Gentle. The Dignity of each and all. Prayerfulness. Not knowing how to pray. Openness. Tranquil Heart. The World is

Injustice. What part of your constant giving does not know its source? (We truly begin when we truly disappear.)

Today's Potatoes? What are you cooking? What am I?...

Dan Novak has been on the faculty at the University of Rhode Island as a part-time instructor for many years. He teaches mainly in the humanities at the URI Alan Shawn Feinstein School of Continuing Education in Providence. He has been active in the University of Rhode Island Chapter of the American Association of University Professors organizing for faculty rights/benefits for part-time members.

Author Index

CPSIA information can be obtained at www.ICGtesting.com
Printed in the USA
BVOW05s2015080814

362232BV00001B/24/P

9 781491 738108